# D R A G

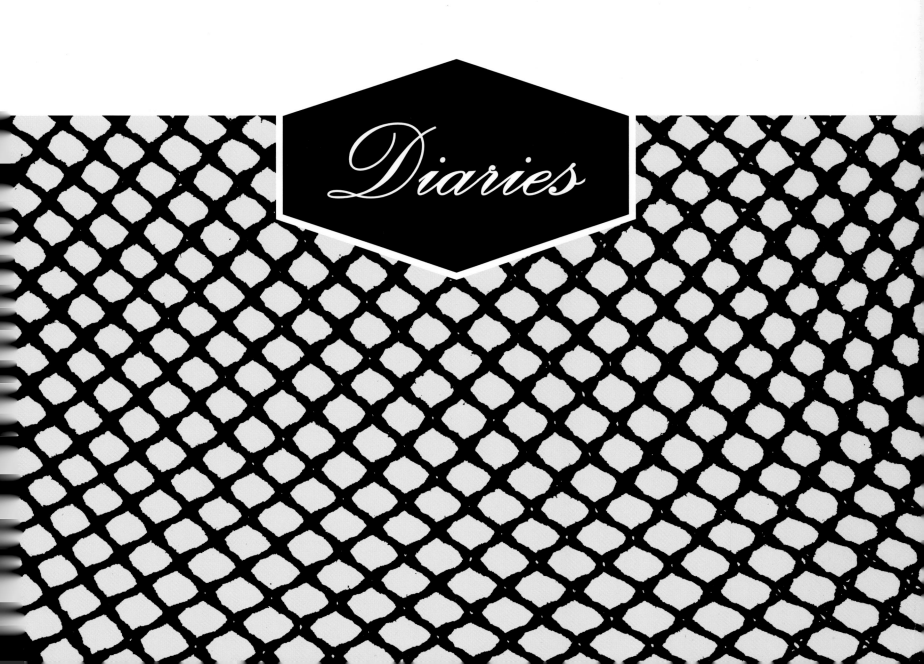

Diaries

# D RAG

*Diaries*

by

CATHERINE CHERMAYEFF

JONATHAN DAVID

and

NAN RICHARDSON

AN UMBRA EDITIONS BOOK

CHRONICLE BOOKS
SAN FRANCISCO

DESIGNED BY

RICK PATRICK FOR
REINER DESIGN CONSULTANTS, NYC

PHOTOGRAPHY BY

WOUTER DERUYTTER
MICHAEL FAZAKERLEY
JESSE FROHMAN
LIZZIE HIMMEL
TOM PITTS
LEN PRINCE
ALBERT SANCHEZ AND
SHONNA VALESKA

PRINTED IN HONG KONG.

EDITED BY NAN RICHARDSON AND CATHERINE CHERMAYEFF

ASSISTANT EDITOR: LEONORA LOWE

BOOK AND JACKET DESIGN BY RICK PATRICK
FOR REINER DESIGN CONSULTANTS, INC.

FIRST EDITION

LIBRARY OF CONGRESS CATALOGING-IN-PUBLICATION DATA
DRAG DIARIES / BY CATHERINE CHERMAYEFF, JONATHAN DAVID, NAN RICHARDSON.
P.   CM.
ISBN: 0-8118-0895-5
1. TRANSVESTITES–INTERVIEWS.  2. TRANSVESTISM–HISTORY.
I. RICHARDSON, NAN,  II. CHERMAYEFF, CATHERINE.  III. TITLE.
HQ77.D38  1995
306.77–DC20
94-37183
CIP

DISTRIBUTED IN CANADA BY RAINCOAST BOOKS,
8680 CAMBIE STREET, VANCOUVER, B.C. V6P 6M9

AN UMBRA EDITIONS BOOK

UMBRA EDITIONS, INC.
180 VARICK STREET
NEW YORK, NEW YORK 10014

10 9 8 7 6 5 4 3 2

CHRONICLE BOOKS
275 FIFTH STREET
SAN FRANCISCO, CALIFORNIA 94103

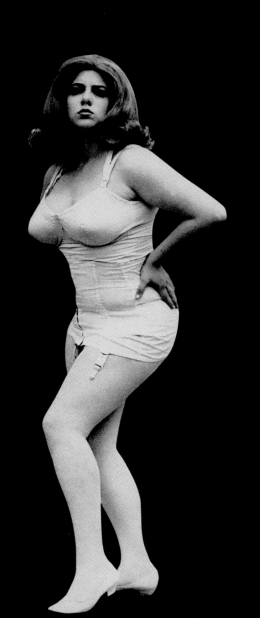

# TABLE OF CONTENTS

# INTRODUCTION

*"WHEN YOU MEET A HUMAN BEING THE FIRST DISTINCTION YOU MAKE IS 'MALE OR FEMALE' AND YOU ARE ACCUSTOMED TO MAKE THE DISTINCTION WITH UNHESITATING CERTAINTY."*

*–Sigmund Freud in* Femininity

Guys have been dressing up as dolls since virtually the beginning of time, from the Greek classical theater to Shakespeare and company, from the transvestite balls of the French Belle Epoch to Dustin Hoffman's *Tootsie.* While females played by men have long been a staple of society, even while skirting its outer limits, the myth of the drag queen, once a category reserved for the dysfunctional, has been given a lively career-gal gloss in the '90s, as drag rises to prominence like no other era, spurred on by a new openness and voyeurism in sexuality, hallmark of the post-AIDS era.

*Drag Diaries* is a door to the world of drag, from its surprisingly rich and varied past to its irreverent, witty, campy present. The term "drag" itself is hardly new. By the 1800s it was in common use, referring to the swish or "drag" of a woman's dress on the ground. It has always had unlikely proponents: Achilles, the great hero of the *Iliad,* Homer's bestselling poem-novel of the 8th century B.C., did a turn in his Grecian gown, and his compatriots regularly played women on the stage. The Romans carried on the tradition for both secular and religious reasons, a heritage kept up by English theater until the sixteenth century: who could forget Alexander Cooke as Lady Macbeth and Robert Goffe as Juliet? The same principle continues to this day in the East, with the mesmerizing illusion and artifice of Noh and Kabuki actors.

On the more contemporary stage, the art of the great pretenders in skirts flourished at the turn of the century with famous vaudeville and burlesque talents like Julian Eltinge and Charles Ruggles, and more recently with comedians like Benny Hill and Milton Berle. Not to be overlooked is the tradition, especially in America, of collegiate amateur theatricals, where donning female garb has been a staple of performance, from Harvard's Hasty Pudding on to the heartland. From the English Pantomime Dame to the American minstrel shows, from Native American berdashes (accepted by many tribes as transvestite shamans, a "third sex") to African tribesmen in ceremonial women's garb, possessing special powers to ward off evil spirits, drag runs wide and deep in many cultures.

The very ubiquity of drag allays many of the fears and suspicions it attracts. Some of history's most famous drags are introduced here, including Bonnie Prince Charlie of Scotland, pretender to the English throne, who saved his neck to fight again by disguising himself as a lassie, the Chevalier Charles D'Eon of France (who gave the name "eonism" to crossdressing), the first governor of New York and New Jersey, Lord Cornbury, alias Edward Hyde, who reviewed his troops in a hoop skirt and bonnet, and many more. Even men of the cloth subscribed: when the Abby de Choisy appeared bejeweled and bewigged in his evening gown at the court of the King of Siam, the natives thought it was some new European fashion.

Drag debunks some of gender's most cherished beliefs. Prior to World War One, for example, baby boys wore pink ("a stronger, more decided color") and girls wore blue (thought to be "delicate" and "dainty"), and it wasn't until the 1940s that the color switch occurred. In fact, for hundreds of years, boys and girls were dressed alike, in frocks, and the ritual threshold of manhood, known as "breeching," marked the move to pants, and later, from short pants to long. The sexualizing of color has made many hairpin turns in

ts history. In 1909, homosexuals were known by their red neckties (according to the Chicago Vice Commission and sexologist Havelock Ellis in his study of New York and Philadelphia). This might be news to Dan Rather, Peter Jennings, and their colleagues. The Nazis used pink triangles to denote "deviants," while by the 1950s green had supplanted red as the gay shade. Nowadays, it's lavender that rules. All of which is to say that culture is a flux variable in the fascination with drag. And drag at its most self-aware revels in the ironies and parodies of social and sexual identity.

But the story of drag in the West is particularly, and most brilliantly, bound up with the story of homosexuality and gay identity, and its importance within gay culture. The other worlds of crossdressing are many and varied and personal; we have chosen largely to leave them outside the scope of this book, even though they may be inspired by some of the same instinctual yearnings. The desire for a space of possibility between the sexes, for a blurring of rigid gender lines, for a redefinition of roles that may be confusing, can be crisis-causing, but ultimately, can be liberating and just plain fun. For there are still penalties for those who risk questioning those boundaries—discrimination and stigmatization have been the rule, rather than the exception. But the pleasure, the power of drag will out, in spite of, perhaps because of, repression by mainstream society. It plays to something primal; the titillation of humor, the fascination of surprise, and some deeper search for meaning. Or perhaps its lure is even more basic; as Colette said, "the seduction emanating from a person of uncertain or dissimulated sex is powerful."

So enter the sulfurous soirees of drag, deliriously energized, the Who's Who of hoo-ha, a world of wholesome decadence that resembles Barnum and Bailey more than Sodom and Gomorrah: where "God save the Queen" follows roller-coaster fashion fantasy competitions called "Delusions of Grandeur." Amid this party world, among the night crawlers and the floor shows, are the performers, whose drag today is a major influence on fashion designers, models, stylists, hairdressers, makeup artists, photographers, and any other followers of the international fashion circus. Meet Lypsinka, alias American Ballet Theater pianist John Epperson, who models himself on a minor Forties screen star named Dolores Gray, with a nod to Joan Crawford. Learn the makeup secrets of two other style queens, Mathu and Zaldy, mannequin/transvestites for the Nineties in platform shoes, and rubber-slick peekaboo bodysuits with a space-age reference. Witness Joey Arias's "channeling" relationship with Lady Day, where performance reaches astral heights.

Follow their days and nights, their elaborate dress-up rituals, their perspective on what the new interest in drag means, supplemented by photographs from their private diaries, in this inside look at a hitherto closed-doors world that has come out of the closet with doors banging in the last two years and entered the mainstream as never before.

—Nan Richardson

# DRAG HISTORY

*1.* Among Native American tribes, transvestites were given status as an honorary third sex. These "berdashes" wore women's clothes and engaged in feminine activities. Cross-dressing was widely documented among the Aztecs, Incas, and Egyptians, among other great civilizations of the past, and exists today in tribal ceremonies around the world. Among the Namshi, for instance, boys are dressed in skirts during rites of initiation, while Masai youths wear women's clothes after circumcision until their wounds heal. Kathakali dancers in Ceylon adorn themselves in jewels and makeup to call up the gods, Zulus to call down the rains, while Indian Bhoota dancers dress as women to ward off evil spirits.

*2.* "Iron Mike" Ames, football megastar, puffs away nonchalantly on his cigarette, 1927.

*3.* Born Vander Clyde in Round Rock, Texas, in 1904, Barbette made his debut as a female trapeze artist at the Harlem Opera House, undetected as a man until he removed his wig at the end of the performance. In 1923 Barbette came to Paris, hailed by the intellectual world led by Jean Cocteau as "a theatrical masterpiece, an angel, a flower, a bird."

*4.* Cabaret for women (attired as men) in Paris's Montmartre district, circa 1930.

5. IN JAPANESE THEATER, DRAG DIVIDES THE KABUKI AND NOH DRAMAS. NOH DERIVES FROM *DENGAKU,* A FOLK DANCE ASSOCIATED WITH RICE PLANTING AND FERTILITY, AND IN ITS ANCIENT, SELF-ENCLOSED SPIRITUAL WORLD, "FEMALE" ACTORS WEARING MASKS FOLLOW STYLIZED ROUTINES IN A COMPLEX AND RAREFIED PATTERN OF SYMBOLIC GESTURES. KABUKI, A LATER FORM DATING FROM THE SEVENTEENTH CENTURY, IS MORE POPULAR AND LESS RITUALISTIC THAN NOH. THERE FEMALE IMPERSONATORS, OR *ONNAGATA,* ARE CAREFULLY MADE-UP, SPEAK IN FALSETTO VOICES, AND MOVE TO SUGGEST THE ESSENCE OF FEMININITY WITH SUCH SUCCESS THAT WOMEN WATCH THE PERFORMANCES IN ORDER TO LEARN DEPORTMENT. THIS IS A PRINT BY TOSHUSAI SHARAHU OF ACTOR OGASAWARA TSUNEYO IN KABUKI COSTUME.

6. JULIAN ELTINGE, BORN JULIAN DALTON IN 1883, FIRST DRESSED AS A WOMAN AT THE AGE OF ELEVEN, BECOMING THE MOST FAMOUS FEMALE IMPERSONATOR OF ALL TIME. ELTINGE SPENT UP TO TWO HOURS BEFORE EACH PERFORMANCE TRANSFORMING HIM- SELF, A PROCESS THAT INCLUDED THE PARTICULARLY PAINFUL PRACTICE OF SHAVING HIS FINGERS. FROM VAUDEVILLE TO THE SILVER SCREEN HE BROKE BOX OFFICE RECORDS IN SHOWS LIKE *THE COUNTESS CHARMING* AND *THE CLEVER MRS. CARFAX.*

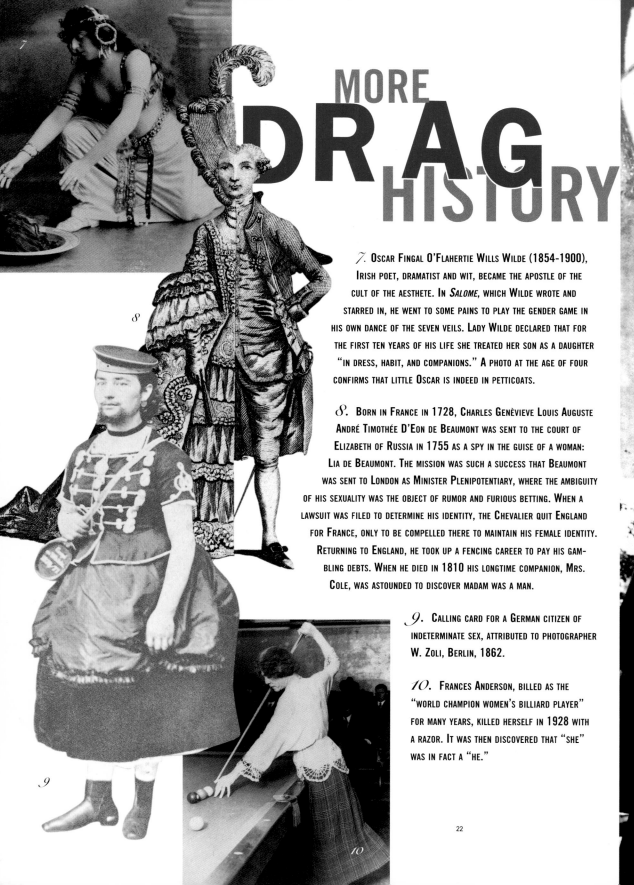

# MORE DRAG HISTORY

*7.* Oscar Fingal O'Flahertie Wills Wilde (1854–1900), Irish poet, dramatist and wit, became the apostle of the cult of the aesthete. In *Salome*, which Wilde wrote and starred in, he went to some pains to play the gender game in his own dance of the seven veils. Lady Wilde declared that for the first ten years of his life she treated her son as a daughter "in dress, habit, and companions." A photo at the age of four confirms that little Oscar is indeed in petticoats.

*8.* Born in France in 1728, Charles Genèvieve Louis Auguste André Timothée D'Eon de Beaumont was sent to the court of Elizabeth of Russia in 1755 as a spy in the guise of a woman: Lia de Beaumont. The mission was such a success that Beaumont was sent to London as Minister Plenipotentiary, where the ambiguity of his sexuality was the object of rumor and furious betting. When a lawsuit was filed to determine his identity, the Chevalier quit England for France, only to be compelled there to maintain his female identity. Returning to England, he took up a fencing career to pay his gambling debts. When he died in 1810 his longtime companion, Mrs. Cole, was astounded to discover madam was a man.

*9.* Calling card for a German citizen of indeterminate sex, attributed to photographer W. Zoli, Berlin, 1862.

*10.* Frances Anderson, billed as the "world champion women's billiard player" for many years, killed herself in 1928 with a razor. It was then discovered that "she" was in fact a "he."

**11.** Seen before and after, Christine Jorgensen exploded fifties complacency about gender when she had a transsexual operation in 1952 and changed from George W. to her now-famous female identity. The Christine Jorgensen story spawned debate and discussion about the hitherto unspoken conviction of biologically normal men and women who felt they were, in reality, members of the opposite sex.

**12.** The Sisters of Perpetual Indulgence are a San Francisco theater group whose revues advocate gay and feminist rights. Among the names in the order, past and present, are Sister Opiate of the Masses, Sister Superior Posterior, Sister Share and Cher Alike, Sister Nocturnal Omissions, Sister Florence Nightmare, Sister Sadie the Rabbi Lady, and more. One star member, Sister Boom Boom (a.k.a. Jack Fertig), ran for city office in 1982 as "Nun of the Above."

**13.** In one of the more famous drag interludes in military annals, Charles Edward Stuart, known as "Bonnie Prince Charlie," 1720-1788, headed the disastrous Jacobite rising in Scotland only to be crushed by Cumberland at Culloden Moor. For five months, before he fled to Brittany, Charlie hid in the Highlands disguised as a woman to escape his enemies.

**STILL EVEN MORE**

*14.* The Duke of Gloucester, aged three, in girls' clothes. Cross-dressing comes in many forms, large and small. Boy babies were frequently called by girls' names to ward off demons, and all over Europe boys were not officially counted until they were "breeched" at age seven, and thereby allowed to wear men's pants and become part of the male world. Until then, boys' hair was coiffed like girls', and dresses were the daily costume. This prudent custom applied to all classes. Family portraits from the sixteenth to the nineteenth centuries identify boys by the toys they carry (whips or wooden horses rather than dolls), and well into the nineteenth century sturdy farmer's lads aged six or more are shown photographed in skirts. The practice even lasted in some places until 1914.

*15.* Television brought female impersonation back to a mass audience with Milton Berle as its biggest attraction. Berle was even featured on the cover of *Newsweek* in 1949 dressed as Carmen Miranda. Explaining his mass appeal he said, "Gay is just another way of life."

# STILL, EVEN MORE
# DRAG
# HISTORY

*16.* SINCE 1844, THE HASTY PUDDING CLUB AT HARVARD HAS BEEN PRESENTING ANNUAL THEATRICALS OF MEN IN SKIRTS. NOT QUITE AS OLD AS THE PUDDING, BUT AS FERVENTLY UPHOLDING OF CROSS-DRESSING RITUALS, ARE THE PAINT AND POWDER CLUB OF BALTIMORE (1898), BOSTON'S TAVERN CLUB (1897), AND THE BOHEMIAN CLUB OF SAN FRANCISCO (1872), KNOWN FOR ITS ANNUAL WEEKEND FROLICS IN THE "BOHEMIAN GROVE."

*17.* BUSTER KEATON, SEEN HERE IN *DOUGHBOYS* (1930), RAISED THE COMEDIC TEMPERATURE WHEN IN WOMEN'S CLOTHING, AS DID PERFORMERS LIKE DANNY KAYE, JERRY LEWIS, GROUCHO MARX, AND THE THREE STOOGES.

*18.* LIKE HIS AMERICAN CONTEMPORARY CHARLES PIERCE (WHOSE ACT SOARS WITH DRAMATIC VULGARITY MADE HEROIC), ENGLISH IMPERSONATOR DANNY LARUE USES THE IMPERFECTION OF DRAG'S "READABILITY" (IN SPITE OF THE METICULOUS ILLUSION OF FEMININITY AND GLAMOUR) TO CREATE A DRAG THAT'S PROFOUNDLY AND UNTHREATEN-INGLY COMIC.

*19.* AUSTRALIAN COMEDIAN BARRY HUMPHRIES'S CREATION, DAME EDNA EVERAGE, IS A DIZZY MATRON WHOSE SCATHING SATIRICAL PARODY OF THE NOBLE BRITISH CONSERVATIVE TRADITION TAKES NO PRISONERS.

*20.* PROBABLY THE MOST FAMOUS NINETEENTH-CENTURY CROSS-DRESSING CASE WAS THAT OF TWO YOUNG MEN OF SOCIETY FAMILIES, ERNEST BOULTON AND FREDERICK PARK, KNOWN POPULARLY AS STELLA AND FANNY. THEY WERE ARRESTED OUTSIDE THE STRAND THEATRE ON APRIL 28, 1870, ELABORATELY DRESSED IN WOMEN'S CLOTHES. WHEN CHARGED AT BOW STREET POLICE STATION WITH "CONSPIRACY TO COMMIT A FELONY," BOULTON'S MOTHER TESTIFIED THAT HER SON "HAD DRESSED AS A GIRL SINCE AGE SIX, AND HIS FAVORITE ROLE WAS AS PARLOR MAID." YOUNG ERNEST'S EXCURSIONS IN BUSTLES CAME TO BE SEEN BY THE PUBLIC AS HARMLESS DIVERSIONS, AND THE YOUNG MEN WERE EVEN-TUALLY ACQUITTED.

# JEM

*The East Side apartment looks uncannily like a Barbie boudoir: pink walls, pink bed, pink lamps, and in the adjoining neat-as-a pin study, row upon row of wigs of rainbow hues and dozens of boat-sized glittery evening shoes. But James O'Connor-Taylor, a.k.a. Jem Jender, is dressed like a nice conservative boy in pressed blue jeans and tucked-in tee shirt.*

I STARTED PERFORMING (NOT NECESSARILY IN DRAG) WHEN I WAS IN THE SECOND GRADE. IT WAS A NICE PRODUCTION OF SNOW WHITE AND THE SEVEN DWARFS. OF COURSE I PLAYED THE PRINCE, BUT I WAS EYEING SNOW WHITE'S DRESS DURING THE WHOLE THING. THAT GAVE ME THE TASTE OF BEING UP ON STAGE AND I SAID, "GEE, I REALLY LIKE THIS." OF COURSE, MY MOM WAS A DANCER AND ON HER SIDE OF THE FAMILY THERE WERE LOADS OF MUSICIANS; MY GRANDFATHER WAS A PIANIST. SO MAYBE IT WAS IN THE GENES THAT I STARTED IN THE THIRD GRADE WITH TAP LESSONS AND THEN ANNUAL DANCE RECITALS. OF COURSE, I WAS THE ONLY BOY AND THIS WAS NEW HAMPSHIRE, SO IT WAS A LITTLE BIZARRE. I REMEMBER CARRYING MY TAP SHOES IN MY LUNCH BOX AND SAYING, "OH MY GOD, I HOPE NO ONE SEES THAT I HAVE LITTLE BLACK TAP SHOES WITH BELL-TONE CAPEZIO TAPS ON THEM." WHEN WE STARTED TO LOOK FOR A SCHOOL, THERE WERE, AT THE TIME, ONLY TWO IN THE UNITED STATES FOR KIDS WITH SERIOUS BALLET TRAINING PLUS ACADEMICS. ONE WAS THE NORTH CAROLINA SCHOOL OF

R

the Arts. So I went down on my first airplane flight ever and met friends I knew from summer theater there. They were actually involved with the PTL (Praise The Lord) club and studying at Heritage USA. They were all born-again Christians. I stayed with them at the PTL club, and actually got to go to Jim Bakker's office and jump in his hot tub. That was kind of a big shake at thirteen! After auditioning I flew back to New Hampshire and ran to the mailbox every single day waiting to see if I got accepted. And I did! So I packed my bags and left.

By then, everyone I knew in New Hampshire had realized that I was defiantly different. I mean, I ran around from October to December wearing—was it the Pink Panther? No, it was a Bugs Bunny costume. I never took it off. Then I was Batman for a long time, running around in a little cape. My mother was very cool, saying, "Do what ever you want to do. We'll go grocery shopping and you can fly up and down the aisles and pick out your breakfast cereal." She knew I was different—not just like the normal kid going out for baseball and track. My mom was just one of the great, great mothers. If I wanted to paint all over the walls of my bedroom, she'd say, "Go to it...here's the paint."

For my dad it was different. My father was more interested in teaching me how to shoot rifles and go out hunting. I remember when he gave me my first .22: "Oh boy." He wanted to make me be as masculine as possible, buying me motorcycles (the first one was a Honda 50, which I *did* enjoy), buying me boxing gloves, while my mother was out buying me ballet slippers. A lot of things Dad taught me that I didn't appreciate when I was a kid I'm certainly glad that I know now. I think he just didn't want to see me go into the world and be discriminated against, be the person that I turned out to be, mostly because he was afraid. He knew that it would be difficult for me, because I wasn't what society accepted, I wasn't the WASPy boy from New England who shoots and

hunts and goes hiking and loves camping and winds up at Harvard with a law degree. I mean, it just wasn't really in the *cards* for me. Our house was always a constant battle over whether I would go to ballet class or skiing or gymnastics.

I had two other brothers who are a lot older than I. My brother Dennis ended up joining the Air Force and got involved with the military (which my dad was thrilled about), and my brother Walt is just very quiet, into getting a new Harley and brewing his beer. He's great, sort of like Norm on *Cheers*.

Our family after my father died and my mother remarried was sort of like *The Brady Bunch*. There are eight of us. My sister Jennifer was the youngest (she passed away, at eighteen) and then Kenny and then me. My sister Kim comes after, then Mark, then Walter, then Dennis and then Renny and Marsha and Greg.

The first time my mother met my dad, well, my step-dad (but I really consider him my father), he was in drag—which I think is just hysterical. He's a very New England man, real popular in the area, and the local Elks Lodge was doing kind of a beauty pageant, a Hasty Pudding thing with all the guys dressed up as beauty pageant contestants. My mother was sitting in the audience with my real father, who was still alive at that point. An associate of my mother's from her bank was involved and when my step-dad said he needed a stage name, this friend mentioned my mom— and so he went out and he announced himself as my mother. It caused a big scandal. My father grabbed her and said, "How do you know that man who's up there in a dress?" After the show my mother met my stepfather for the first time. (Kind of sweet, isn't it?)

My influences as a kid were Disney, musical theater, ballets, and seeing old movies, like Fred and Ginger; I think we're all victims of that. Just looking at all that old Hollywood stuff I would sort of escape, fantasizing, "Well God, I would love to be

# I am <u>am</u> shy

a Busby Berkeley girl tap-dancing all over Central Park." Then I wanted to be Farrah Fawcett when *Charlie's Angels* was on. That was that teenage point when all of a sudden you look in the mirror and go, "YUCK, I hate the way I look."

But first, I had to get *out* of New Hampshire. You have to picture this: we lived on a dirt road in a small country town called Plaistow. Hale Spring Road actually had a natural spring and people came from all over to pump water out of the spring and fill up their jugs. It was about as country as you can get. I knew there was nothing there for me.

So, I moved to New York, which caused a big drama between my mother and me. She pretty much put her foot down, and said she wasn't going to support me. So here I was, sixteen years old, with no place to live, and no money. The first couple of months were very difficult. I remember three of us living off a banana. It was all we could afford so we'd divide it up and then go to Robert Denvers and take class. *Everything* was just ballet—I was a nun for years. I called myself a black-and-white TV because all I did was go to American School of Ballet, wear a white tee shirt, a pair of black tights, and white shoes. Dancers, at that point in my life, were the ones that influenced me: Patricia McBride (how beautiful and elegant she was), Heather Watts, and Suzanne Farrell. I was like a little sponge saying, "When I get on stage I am going to do it *exactly* like that."

My mother forgave me after I appeared in *LIFE* magazine in a really nice story about the School of American Ballet. She got it then—she realized what I was doing. At that point all I ever *dreamed* about was being in New York City Ballet. For three years I just trained and trained, living in a quadrangle between my health club, a job in Lincoln Center, school, and my apartment on 60th Street. I had no idea what was going on in the world, only what the company was performing that night. I had no idea who was running for the president of the United States—and didn't care. In ballet, you are totally focused, blinders on—nothing else matters. Your mind goes completely blank and you don't think about anything except your exercises at

the bar, the right turn out and the right line. Even now when I go to ballet classes, I can be having a completely stressful day and the pianist starts and my left hand hits the bar, and I think about *nothing* else. As a discipline it's wonderful—a sort of meditation process.

After the School of American Ballet I just sort of stopped, didn't want to dance at all. I ended up having an accident where I became paralyzed, losing the use of my left side. My mother took me to countless neurologists up in Boston and I had to learn to speak again: b's and p's were especially difficult. I spent about six months at my parents' house just getting it back together. I would swim, exercise, sit in front of a mirror and get my lips to work, get my vowels going. One day I was just lounging out by the pool when my mother came up to me and said, "Jimmy? Don't you think it's time you get back to New York and get on with it?" I said "Yeah—I'd better go...."

I had to make a decision. I enjoyed my life in the city and being part of New York. Still, I was just about ready to pack up my bags and move down to Atlanta when I got a call from the Ballet Trocadero of Monte Carlo. I was living with my friend Tanya, who said, "Jimmy, they want to sign you up and give you a contract! It's health insurance and a good salary—what about it?" I remember thinking, "That involves gluing on eye-lashes and putting on a wig, putting on point shoes and being a *ballerina*." But Tanya pushed: "It's a ticket around the world!" So I said "Right—I'll see the world!"

What Ballet Trocadero does is a parody of all the ballet classics, bringing a sense of humor to the choreography and to the style. We're all dressed as ballerinas and we're all sort of making fun of it but at the same time we're out there doing the actual original choreography. I mean *Swan Lake* was a bitch every night! My feet were constantly bleeding, I was losing toenails, seeing a podiatrist every week. Hard, grueling work— and also comedy. Through that I realized that I was a pretty good comedian and I could get a couple thousand people to laugh without even opening my mouth—with everything through dance. It was all so foreign to me: I had no idea how to even put on lipstick (I'd done theatrical makeup, but now I had these *eyelashes*). Everyone in the company helped me at the beginning with a bit of this and that. I look at those photographs now and I just want to vomit. Oh, my God—you've come a long way, girl!

Overall, I've performed in every state in America, except North Dakota and Hawaii. I've been to every city in France,

Europe during the fall, the United States during the winter, and spring and summer in Japan. I was seeing all these places I learned about in art history: cave art in Lascaux, the Mona Lisa at the Louvre. Of course, it seems really glamorous but it really isn't because all you're doing is working. You get off an airplane, someone picks you up, you drop your luggage at the hotel, you go right to the theater, you have a company class and then rehearse what wasn't good in the performance the night before. You do the show, you go out to dinner, you go to bed, and then you do it all over again.

Of course, you lose any kind of a life. I would just come home to my apartment, put down my bags and collapse and sleep for a day. Then I would have to get back to ballet classes, pack and go again.

That is all I did for five years. When we did really big tours there were about eighteen of us. It was tight knit, with certain programs that sort of ran like clockwork. We all had different backgrounds, with one similarity: ballet training. But oh God, we were always all at each other's throats. Put twelve drag queens on a plane together with everyone with such different personalities. My God, the fights, the bickering, the arguments! But when it got right down to it, at show time the curtain went up and all was forgotten. After the show, when the curtain closed people marched off to their dressing rooms

in their tutus and the daggers were flying, and all the bitching started again.

Then, after I was approached to do a film called *Rude Awakening*, I started to get a lot of attention—because I was always the pretty one, and actually *looked* like a woman out there. Most of the guys are very big, big guys, six feet tall with hairy chests and makeup. At that point, my makeup was still very exaggerated, with big eyebrows and big lips, but from the stage I just looked like a ballerina. And after that film (with Cheech and Eric Roberts) I said, "God, I really *like* this kind of work." So I hooked up with an agency and they sent me out to play drag queens. Soon I began to get other projects (a commercial or print ad or shooting with different photographers) and shy away from the company. That caused a bit of hostility. What really frosted the cake was when I published my own book, which I sold on the tour. I ended up going on vacation and sitting on an island and saying, "Oh my God, I've got to go back in a week and those drag queens are gonna *kill* me."

One day I came home to a message on my answering machine from a Swiss woman, Susanne Bartsch, with the strangest accent: "I tink dat you're vonderful, and I vant you to come and vork for me at the Copacabana." I'd never been to a nightclub but decided to give it a try. I walked into the dressing room and couldn't believe what I was seeing. All the costumes and the color, all the different personalities! I said, "Oh my God, all this has been going on and I don't know *anything about it*! I was very scared at first. But I eased right into it and the rest is history. It was energy like I had never seen before in my life and I was a virgin to it all. All my dancing life had been *so* controlled (you know Russian ballet teachers), so *directed*. When I stepped into the Copa I saw all these people who were totally free artistically, and everyone seemed happy. There were no criticisms, no notes. It was totally up to me. I think that was the first time I ever allowed myself to be creative with who I was. That's where I developed Jem Jender and who *she* is. And it was at those parties that I found drag.

Anthony Wong once said to me: "If you think you've gone

too far just keep on going." What's great about drag—what I cherish about it, is that I have a balance in my life. I'm really just a shy boy from New Hampshire with a ballet background, but when I put on a blond wig and strap myself into a corset with an eighteen-inch waist and size-twelve Vivienne Westwood heels, I become a different person. It's a treat—I wish everyone could do it! And I couldn't live any other way.

I was thinking the other day that I've never had an unpleasant experience in drag. When I go out in drag it's always to a party or an event—a fundraising event for AIDS, a fashion shoot, a film, a commercial. It's always a wonderful and happy experience. Look, you're not going to wake up in the morning, put on a wig and a pair of high heels and go argue with the IRS! It becomes an addiction, because you're *guaranteed* a good time, and *guaranteed* happiness. Hey—when you go to an amusement park, you go on the rides!

I should add that I have no interest in becoming a woman. I worship women and enjoy personifying them, but being one? Oh God, no thanks! I don't want to drag around

breasts twenty-four hours a day. God bless women! (I think that needs to be made clear.)

Drag-wise, I wasn't a drag queen; I was an actor playing a role. Being Jem Jender allows me to do and say things I wouldn't otherwise say or do as a man. It's an entirely different person. I cherish Jem Jender. She doesn't do anything bad— she's not a bad girl. She represents a kind of freedom that I don't have as James O'Connor-Taylor. I drop all kinds of boundaries that I set for myself as a man. Now, of course, it's become a business, a celebrity person that I become. But it's been a three-year process. Now I know exactly who Jem Jender is, what she thinks and what she does.

What's fun about my character is that I can go anywhere and get people to laugh and smile. My drag is very unthreatening to people because it's bright and colorful, like a Disney cartoon character. People are comfortable around it because I'm so comfortable doing it.

My Dad always says: "James, when you enter a room make sure everyone knows who you are and where you're

coming from." I've taken that to heart—I enter a room like a bright light. It's fun to find the shy person in the corner and loosen them up, get their energy going. And it's my *job*. When I do parties for Armani, my job is to bring the energy level up. Dear God, I *am* shy as can be. As a boy I *never* go out. I went to the Art Dealers' show the other night. I went in a suit and tie, and just stood there with my glass of champagne. I saw a lot of people there who know Jem Jender but had no idea who I am. I saw Bill Cunningham from *The New York Times* and I went up to him (he's photographed me a million times in drag) and I said, "I'm Jem Jender," and he was *shocked*. He started stuttering. I said, "I left the wig and heels at home." You see, that night I was myself: shy and quiet, minding my business. Maybe because I don't get to go out as a man anymore, I'm out of practice being James O'Connor-Taylor. I compare myself to characters like Mae West—people who are so busy portraying their characters that you think that's who they really are. Off the stage I'm sure she was an entirely different person. It's important to take a little distance and keep James O'Connor-

Taylor in mind. It's a performer's hazard—you forget the base and the source of the whole thing.

Right now you are in a Christian home. Really. God's watching over you. But seriously, I *am* a Christian and God and Jesus Christ are really important figures in my life. I keep going back to my mother, but she was an important influence. She encouraged me to explore all kinds of religion. I went to Hebrew School with my best friend, Paul Goldberg, and my first girlfriend, Cindy Segal, with whom I passed notes back and forth at Temple Emmanu-El in Haverhill, Massachusetts. I explored Catholicism. I also went through a phase where I didn't believe in God: my "atheist teenager trying to figure it all out" period.

My religion affects everything. I know where I'm going and where I'm coming from and that everything happens for a reason. Bad experiences happen for a reason: God is showing me something I need to change. In the drag world, my religion keeps me out of the gossip. People don't have a bad thing to say about me and I don't have a bad thing to say about anyone

else. It sounds a little saccharin, like a contestant in a beauty pageant, but it's very difficult. It's harder to not say anything bad. It's constant work.

Being a Christian is part of my life. I don't pass judgment on people. And who am I to pass judgment? I'm living a very different life. I wouldn't throw stones at anybody, but there are so many people out there that throw stones at me because of how I live and my lifestyle. Through this, my family is a great support system, they're wonderful. I love them and they love me. Especially my mother, who is the vice-president of Bay Banks. She was Business Woman of the Year, she's a Lady Lion, she raises funds for the March of Dimes and she's active with the church. She has always told me to do what makes me happy and she's never withdrawn her support. I'm sure somewhere in her mind it would be easier for her if I were a doctor or a lawyer; but at this point she's surrendered. When my sister Jennifer died at eighteen from diabetes, she realized that our visit on earth is short. The first time I did a daytime talk show I called her to let her know. After all, she lives in a conservative town and has a conservative business life. I don't want to hurt my family in any way, or make them uncomfortable. But actually, my family loves it. They know I'm not in a corset and wig at Foodtown first thing in the morning. My brother, Walter, carries a photo of me in his wallet and shows it to the guys. My grandmother saw me the first time in drag when I was doing *Swan Lake* and she came up to me after the show with tears in her eyes and said: "You looked prettier than your mother on her wedding day."

America is a young country and our drag culture hasn't evolved that far yet. But now drag is brand new in a bigger public way. People weren't ready for *Tootsie* or RuPaul but now America's getting it and starting to enjoy it. That said, I consider myself a pioneer. I want to set a good example so that future generations can build on the drag tradition. I'm not saying that there are going to be scholarship programs in corset making or wig styling, but there's recognition. I'm not the first, but I'm the first of many.

My grandmother saw me the first time in drag when I was doing *Swan Lake* and she came up to me after the show with tears in her eyes and said: "You looked prettier than your mother on her wedding day."

L

*The huge Soho loft is awash in pale pink light, and the dulcet waves of Mendelssohn strings mingle with the burble of the tea kettle as Lavinia, a.k.a. Vincent Meehan, rustles through a forest of tulle and ribbons to find a particular fairy godmother costume he created. Scrubbed of all makeup, his fine-boned face looks ascetic, spiritual, and his gentle voice and fluid grace as he offers up sugar cookies and cream with our cuppa speak more of a priest or geisha than of his legendary force as a founding member of Bloolips, the radical gay theater ensemble.*

My goal is to make people feel comfortable about drag—not formal drag but theatrical suggestions, bits and pieces of garbage woven together to look right. In this definition of drag, appearance is all about illusion. Drag was never about female impersonation. It's about the feminine principle in the male. There's emphatically the feminine and masculine within the male. I'm not trying to be a female, not at all. I'm trying to bring out the feminine principle within me—and not deny it, and not deny my maleness as well. There's two sides of you—the Yin and the Yang. It's all in your head, and my drag uses glitter and tinsel and fantasy makeups to express this.

When you put on a character you can go and do whatever you like. But not only through dressing up as a character. It's also about finding the comedian in you, developing your personal stage persona. It's not about *impersonation*. Who is Lavinia? Lavinia is a *persona* that comes out of me, but Lavinia's goal is simply to be the source of her own material. It comes from *me*, it's got *me* in it, but I can't really say *what I am*. When I dress up I'm not looking toward tits, but my drag might have the feel of tits, of the feminine. It's certainly very colorful, and it has a sense of humor. I think people respond to me chiefly as a clown. Kids, especially, relate to the whole thing very well. Normal people get confused: "Is it a drag queen? But she's got all this glitter and white face, so it's not *exactly* drag." Good—I try to avoid stereotypes. You've got to find your own expression, and mine is more about comedy, about stand-up, about developing a persona for the stage than anything else. Look at Jack Benny, and his unique droll way. He developed that—it's part of him. I see drag in the same way. It's about comedy and finding a persona, even if it's a female persona (which is an aspect of drag; I'm not denying that).

There is a difference, though, from absolute impersonation all the way through to being absolutely male with a very feminine side. Drag is

## IT'S A MASK

what you wear: "The Drag (sic)." It was called drag because it was a dress that you dragged along. You had a train. So drag to me is costume—it's what you wear. So in the gay thing the whole butch look is really just drag. When I said to Thierry Mugler: "Love your drag," he didn't like that—I think he associated drag with something female. But to me it's costume, it's what you wear. You can't always be "as a male," in that one role. I find it dull always wearing the same clothes, the same drag, as a male.

Drag gives me comfort—it's a mask. People want to associate it with the female impersonator, because that's old, it's known, it's safe. But where

I'm going is experimental. It looks like a woman? It *is* a woman. Others are sickened by it, it plays to them as freaky because they can't hang their coat on it. In fact, it's about many things, including playing with all aspects of costumes and design, about exploring the sensuousness of fabrics and colors.

There were loads of comedians who did drag as part of their comedy in England. Dick Emory and Monty Python, for instance, use drag all the time. Benny Hill did drag. There's a big comedy tradition with the English and Irish which is really centered around language. They haven't a national costume or dance but they definitely have a national language.

And although there's an acceptance of drag in England and Ireland because of the pantomime tradition, there's a middle-America in England, too. They don't quite go for it, because drag is always associated with being gay. Even Edna Everage, a straight man with two children, had to work very hard. The English didn't like this Australian who has a very objective eye, someone who can really see the British as they are and send them up gutless, talking about the queen and all that. The Italians and Spanish deny their gayness publicly, though in family life, it's OK, everyone will accept it. This in contrast to an English family, where it will be completely ignored, never mentioned. The Germans have an old history of cabaret (more like the British in that, really). They have an interesting attitude towards the theater, partly, because of Brecht. They haven't got the musical tradition that England has, but they did start one, a strong one, in the '30s.

As the young Vincent Meehan I always played with girls and I wasn't very good at football. I grew up in a working class neighborhood. My block of flats were very Irish and very Jewish; and these cultures were a very strong influence on me. The Kelleys and the Cohens. And I knew that six million Jews had died when I was five. I

knew I couldn't marry my best friend, Elaine Sugarman, because she was Jewish. (Her father was the porter in the flat). My Jewish friends had the same strong sense of humor like the Irish. Otherwise, it was pretty rough around the neighborhood.

My parents were basically Irish. They came back and forth during the war. The Irish keep it quiet in England. They don't want any trouble, any bother. My Mum and Dad weren't political at all, though I always knew I was Irish, that I was from somewhere green. We took the boat over to Ireland to visit the family now and then.

We were Catholics. I loved dressing up even as an altar boy. That was fun: it's a lovely little outfit. Then I joined the boy scouts. It got me out of London, and it was jolly: knots, cooking, playing in uniforms! At that time the Scouts did a lot of big performances, with hundreds of Scout actors, singers etc., called "The Gang Shows." Huge shows. I played a Chinese boy and once I got a whiff of Pond's Cold Creme I was hooked. Forget the grease paint—that didn't do it. The make-up remover, the cold cream, that was it for me. I also sang in the church. I had a high-pitched voice. I always participated in the nativity. Then there was a core of six of us in school who put on musicals. We had news, and adverts, and jokes. I did about six of these variety shows. What made me happy as a boy was singing in the school, the school plays, the big Christmas pageants—anything to do with theater and performance stayed with me. But all that was secondary in those schools; they just wanted you to learn your academics.

But there were many influences pulling me towards performance. There is, of course, a history to this. All the way through vaudeville you have classic drag acts; in fact, in the '20s and '30s people like Douggie Bing were bigger than Noel Coward. Bing did the whole range of musical comedy: he

...ONCE I GOT A WHIFF OF POND'S COLD CREME, I WAS HOOKED.

played the Ugly Sister; he played the Dame. Pantomime in England goes way back to the Dame, the man in drag. It appears over and over again in vaudeville. Women did it too: Esther Tillie and others. They were often played in drag. Vaudeville drag also includes another female staple: the horrific, horrendous, stereotypical, self-oppressive misogynist view represented by the sisters in Cinderella. Anyway, Bing made more money, was more popular than any actor in his time—and, of course, you've never heard of him! But if in England you had music hall, here you had black acts or minstrel impersonations, along with Jewish acts, even animal acts. Music hall had to speak to and reflect all sorts of people. The world was full of rigid stereotypes so crossover was of interest. Al Jolson really reflects what *white* men wanted: they wanted to be silly. This was their idea of a black man, because they couldn't escape from their straitjacket roles.

As oppressively as this role/gender thing develops (and it did develop to be more oppressive than it originally was), I don't think it was ever meant to be so restrictive. Drag gives men the opportunity to let loose a bit, and then it's interesting to see how a woman emerges on the other side. Look at the way the drag has changed in the Twenties, Thirties, and Forties, along with women's fashions. Skirts got shorter and shorter, shoulder pads came and went, until in the Sixties, a T-shirt and jeans were all women needed. They liberated themselves. There's no need for male impersonators. But there's still a need for female impersonators, because men just can't get over that big bump of wearing a piece of flowing material. Maybe one day it'll all be androgyny, but we're not there yet.

Drag isn't even completely accepted in the gay community.

In the 1890s and early 1900s there were political movements like the Luddites who would have men in drag arrested. It was all very political, because it was upsetting to see a man in drag. Drag is still on the fringes—it's part of gay culture but still on the fringes.

The male playing 'round with the female role will be around a long time in the gay community, because a lot of the gay stuff is about identity crisis. I play around with the male and female role even without being in and out of drag. The masculine principle has dominated the gay scene in the Eighties and Nineties, but the drag thing has been there throughout.

Coming out started for me in the Gay Lib days of 1970–72. It was quite revolutionary back then. A lot of queens were getting on the buses with make-up on, paying their fares and just inviting all the older ladies to be freaked at these men with beards and blue eyeshadow. Though Gay Lib happened here in the States with Stonewall in 1969, it took a few years to get over to England. Gay Lib comes out of the black power movement in the U.S. You know, "Why don't you just go and do it yourself, since no one's going to do it for you." There was a lot of street drag then, but it was all part of a deliberate, politically conscious effort. In the early Seventies, we were hiring town halls and having big gay liberation dances. Then the whole gay liberation movement moved into local areas. In London it was mostly in the west: Notting Hill Gate and Fulham, and the East End of London was way back.

The Gay Lib thing opened up the area of drag and costume and what it was possible to do. I started studying dance when I was about twenty, for about four years. I knew I wanted to be a performer but not necessarily a dancer. But the London School of Contemporary Dance (where I was on a scholarship) didn't want you to play roles, didn't want you to be feminine. They wanted men to be men and women to be women.

I found myself looking at Western dance and thinking "Did I really want to go that way?" Instead I hooked up with Bloolips. Bloolips have been called a lot of things: political theater among them. They wanted to use the ideas that were born during Gay Lib, but at the time the drag queen was still isolated. Drag had never really got any recognition–there was no sense that it was going anywhere politically. It was always: "Don't upset the apple cart." The gay liberals and politicos would say: "We want to be normal, we want to be accepted by society and you come along with these costumes, make-up, and drag, and you put us back." Their idea was to clone everyone—to normal-ize everyone. You see, men want to go towards uniforms, whereas women tend to be diverse. Now, as much as they might compete in their diversity (which is another problem), men in uniform feel comfortable: they belong; they're happy. And this traditional idea, with all its associations, shaped their atti-tudes toward drag.

　　　Whereas Bloolips worked on a clown drag idea. Bloolips was invented by Bette Bourne, who had got her start with a drag theater group in New York called The Hot Peaches. So Bette, influenced by The Hot Peaches, wanted to get some-thing on. But Bette didn't go along entirely with the "Gay Sweatshop" political aspect; he wanted much more of the

# DRAG GIVES MEN THE OPPORTUNITY TO LET LOOSE A BIT, AND THEN IT'S INTERESTING TO SEE HOW A WOMAN EMERGES ON THE OTHER SIDE.

musical comedy. Bette was from Hackney, more of an East End person, even though he did a whole classi-cal training in Shakespeare, and a lot of West End theater. He had come through Gay Lib and dropped out and was very straight. The first show of Bloolips was *The Ugly Duckling.* Simple story: Queen Cockerel and the Mother Duck hate the duckling because she's differ-

ent. Moral: you can do what you want, be who you want. You can come out.

The first year of Bloolips was hard. We did venues around London, at the Oval and the ICA and in Power Square; and once in Bath. We had whittled our group down to seven when we got a booking in Amsterdam for one night and ended up staying for three months. We lived on a boat, pooling our money, with the writer, Jon-Jon. After *The Ugly Duckling* we did *Cheek*, the story of Mary Whitehouse, or Mary Maison Blanche. She was similar to Anita Bryant, same period, and part of the whole right-wing anti-gay thing. We came up with a number like Titty-Bum, sung to the William Tell overture: (singing) "Titty-bum, titty-bum, titty-bum, bum, bum...." We then sang "Bananas": "Oh, Bananas, bananas. They're lovely in tuxedos or pajamas." Then we did our first tap number: "We're in the money, we're in the money," dressed as coins. We were like a herd of horses. The format was like a cabaret musical show. Then we did *Salome*. The main thing wasn't the language, it was the music and the images. It was very visual. After *Vamp and Camp* which used bits from all the shows, Rex and Jon-Jon wrote *Lust In Space.* The "story" began at the Queen's Launderama, where we found Prince Charles's underwear and went to the moon. On the way we did an in-flight number, donning cheese disguises so we wouldn't be seen by the Russians. Just another reason for a costume change, really. There was Edam with a big red lamp shade, and Diva Dan played Cottage Cheese—since "cottage" in English means "toilets," "Cottage Cheese" had a double meaning. I was James Pond, and would come on stage and find a shoe. "Careful, it's a shoe," someone said. "No, it's a plot." I snapped back. "Good, we need one," was the response. Then we had a Nuclear War skit, where Bette did a Yin and Yang number: (Singing) "Somewhere there is a finger of note / That has it's hand on your throat / Nuclear War, Important Finger / I wonder who owns the digit / That makes us humans worry and fidget / To send us all to smithereens / Ronald Reagan or the Queen? / The CIA, the KGB...," and so on.

You see, that's where we put our punch in. We'd do something all smoothly and nicely but there would be a double meaning. It was very Brechtian. It would step right out and start dishing to the audience—bring them right into it. And it was always a mixed audience—you couldn't count on gays only or you wouldn't make enough money. We toured that in the States and then Bette and Rex wrote this story about a pink triangle (like the Bermuda triangle) where all the gays were disappearing. This was in 1983, and at that time, AIDS was still mysterious—we had no idea how symbolic it was. There was a song we did from that called "Tap Your Troubles Away." It went like this: "That rash, you think it's the clap / It keeps comming back, won't go away / When the doctor says: 'Why you'll probably die,'/ Tap your troubles away."

After a while we cut that out. It was very tricky and in the end it was *too* real. The extreme idea of the gay lifestyle was that we'd had sex in every other convoluted way so here we were eating each other, so our skit included a nightclub in the middle of the Pink Triangle where they were putting everyone in pots and boiling them up and eating them. It was supposed to represent this new kind of gay decadence. I did "Think Pink" in the show. It went like this: "Think Pink, on the Yellow road ahead / Red is dead, Blue is through / Green's a bean / And Brown's taboo. / There's not the slightest excuse / For Plum or Puce or Chartreuse / Think Pink...."

After the next show it took a while before we got back together, to do *Living Leg Ends*, based on the Bible. The Old Testament act featured an Adam and Eve where Eve wouldn't eat the apple: "Got any apricots?" *Sunny Sodom on the Sands* was also an Old Testament number. It included all this stuff about sodomy and why we were so preoccupied with it and how it got misinterpreted through the ages. There was a whole hippie trip with Jesus—we just *ran* through the New Testament.

We toured for six months: Germany, Amsterdam, Norway, America. Then the following year we did the life of Madame Mao called *Slung Back and Strapless or Famous Actresses Who Rise to Positions of Power.* The whole thoughts of

Chairman Mao in a minute and a half, and it was marvelous. (Singing): "I was born in a junk on the Hue-Hue river." After *Slung Back and Strapless* we came back to America with *Sticky Buns*, a very off-the-wall, cabaret-style musical. Audiences liked that very much. After that, *Teenage Trash*, a story about the suit in society—how we are all "suitists," and what's "suitable." It was really all about drag.

During those last three years, our shows went on for a full year. Bloolips at that point was me, Diva Dan, Bette Bourne and Pearl. Four of us. Though other people became part of the group for different shows. We were very active; we did the Edinburgh festival, got Arts Council grants, did Leeds, Liverpool, Halifax, and Ottawa. Then Bette wanted to do something but Jon-Jon claimed it was his material and got a lawyer. And that led to the final breakup of the original Bloolips.

Though Bette immediately made another show, I was supportive but I didn't continue. Bette then developed *Get Hur*, which is the story of Hadrian and Antinous. I filled in when they did it in New York, but by the Nineties I had done twelve years of Bloolips. I started a show of my own with Phil, calling ourselves The Fruits (one of a pair). We did a show called the *Globular Choir Disposal Shoot*, the story of a sea which keeps rising, so two internalized oppressed gays have to keep moving inland. He played Philibuster, the first minister, and I was Viscount Vinaigrette, Vin Ordinaire, VSOP, Order of the Bath, Order of the Bucket and a Side Order of Chips. Every time there was a problem we wrote a check and dropped it down the shoot. We started out very pre-historic and as we moved inland, took on a more medieval aspect. We did a song called "Dennis Dildo's Do's and Don'ts" about the Christian Church and how phallic it was. As the sea kept rising we came inland to Industrium. There we did a vaudeville number where we were The Emulsions: Matt Silk and Vinyl Finish. We came even further inland to High Tech Land, and eventually I tried to push Philibuster down the shoot but I fell down and then he fell down by accident and then the Goddess appeared to us and said: "Yes, you are stupid fucked-up men, but you got to get

over it and move on." (A moral message of a kind.) After some cabaret I came to the U.S. to study the Alexander technique and for the last three years did that, during which time I worked for Susanne Bartsch.

Now my performances combine many influences. I continue to address the fact that men are so uptight. When they see me and loosen up, it has a healing aspect. I've often felt when I'm performing that I'm cheering people up: in part just by being an openly outward gay person, who's not in denial. They can see someone out, and gay, and it helps—we don't have to keep *explaining* it. It's going over the hump and laughing at ourselves. It's about making people more comfortable. It breaks them out of their Saturday night best clothes. Drag makes people really *see* themselves—and their attitudes.

I feel bitter that we were gay and though we were part of the sexual revolution, along with women, we are now dying, still under a cloud of prejudice. The sexual political revolution that happened in the Sixties and Seventies was the beginning of Gay Lib, too. Women could have sex because of the pill; they could have sexual freedom and so could gay men. A wider definition seemed possible. But then this change in the gay world occured, and here we are and it's all the same now. My gay culture is being killed by bad attitudes towards us. Early on, when AIDS first hit, the attitude was horrendous towards gays: "They're only gays, it doesn't matter. Let them die." But even now, I'm really, really skeptical of heterosexual viewpoints. I cannot trust them. I'm very hurt. I've got a lot of bitter personal feeling to get over and it will take a while. Historically, it's a long haul between RuPaul and Boy George. Can you come out as a gay performer and have a career, and somewhere to go, and not be pigeonholed? I don't know how long it will take for people to get over their stereotypes about drag….

Interview

*A RECENT TALK OF THE TOWN PIECE IN THE NEW YORKER REFERRED TO JOEY ARIAS AS A "BUCCANEER OF BOHEMIAN STYLE." JOEY, WHO GIVES HIS AGE AS "BETWEEN THIRTY-FIVE AND DEATH," IS A MESMERIZING SINGER WHO EERILY HITS THE HIGH NOTES OF GRIEF AND GLADNESS, MADCAP JOY AND MISCHIEVOUS CHARM AS HE "CHANNELS" BILLIE HOLIDAY OR METAMORPHOSES INTO HIS ALTER EGO, JUSTINE. THE INCREDIBLE, THE GORGEOUS, THE ALCOHOLIC JOEY JOINED US IN OUR WEST SIDE RIV VU OFFICE FOR CAPPUCCINO AND A SUMMER SUNSET.*

JOEY ARIAS

I GUESS THE FIRST TIME I REALLY EVER DRESSED UP (I DIDN'T THINK OF IT AS DRAG), WAS IN THE THIRD GRADE. MY PARENTS WOULD GO TO THE DRIVE-INS, FIVE DAYS A WEEK WHERE THEY WOULD SEE ALL THESE MOVIES (*GYPSY*, *DRACULA*, *THE MUMMY*, *CAN-CAN*). *CLEOPATRA* HIT ME REALLY HARD. THAT VERY NEXT DAY, WHEN MY PARENTS WENT OUT SHOPPING, I GOT TOWELS AND THE NEIGHBORHOOD KIDS AND DID MY EYES UP WITH LOTS OF COLOR, PLAYING CLEOPATRA IN THE HOUSE. MY PARENTS CAME BACK AND FREAKED OUT: I HAD ALL THESE BLACK STATUES AND THE NEIGHBORHOOD KIDS WITH THEIR CLOTHES OFF, AND I HAD THESE FRIENDS OF MINE ON TOP OF ME WHILE I WAS IN THE CHAISE-LOUNGE SPRAWLED ON LEOPARD RUGS. I ALWAYS REMEMBER AS A KID PLAYING AT PORTRAY-ING CHARACTERS FROM DIFFERENT MOVIES. I'D BE THE ONLY WOMAN ON A SHIPWRECKED BOAT AND I'D PUT A BRA ON AND ALL THE GUYS WOULD HUMP ME AND KISS ME OR I WAS THE INDIAN PRINCESS WHEN WE PLAYED COWBOYS AND INDIANS, SO I'D HAVE A LITTLE FRINGE SKIRT ON. YOU SEE, I WAS ALWAYS GAY—AS FAR BACK AS I CAN REMEMBER.

I was born in North Carolina. I'm an Army baby. But my parents moved back to California. I grew up across the street from the *General Hospital* building, from the show. That visual was my horizon. I watched crazy people screaming out of the windows and people running up and down the street nude. What can I say—it was a crazy childhood. My father was a machinist for airplanes and missiles and the space shuttle. My Dad was very laid back. My mom was a housewife. I got all my energy from my mother. She was wild and outgoing and talkative and crazed. Once in the fourth grade, I dyed my hair black and put spots all over it. I didn't do it right. Then I tweezed my eyebrows out and I put Clearasil on my face and powdered it. When they threw me out of school, I came home and my mom was wearing dark glasses (I knew she was angry when she wore dark glasses). She yelled: "What have you done to yourself? Look at your eyebrows! Ahhhhhhh!" She wanted to know, I guess, what would become of me, "Why wasn't I playing sports? Would she have to get me dolls?"

In elementary school I was president of this monster movie club, and I always wore monster make-up to school. The kids hated me but later on, when I graduated, they complimented me and said: "You were always yourself." The monster movie club used to meet in this old abandoned mansion, in the cellar. We always brought the latest monster magazines and cards. Of course, the nuns always caught me with this stuff in school and I'd get punished. I went to Catholic school my whole life. I loved my education. My dad took me to school early so we would

go to morning mass, every day for eight years. I'd walk in and put my sweater over my head and pray with thirty nuns in front of me. I loved ceremonies. That whole Latin thing with all the nuns bowing on the floor, and rituals and robes and fabrics and adoring things: I loved it all.

So I graduated and went to a Catholic boys' school, where

I was always in trouble. People were making fun of me for swishing. I'd try to fit in with the guys but I really didn't. I was into imitating songs and singing. I'd get other boys to dance and I'd do the choreography. I'd do my little show. Movies and TV were a big influence as was anything Japanese. *The Nun's Story* with Audrey Hepburn is one of my favorites. To get rid of us our parents would send me to the movies during the summer. I'd go every day and watch the same movie. I saw *Gypsy* twice a day for two weeks. I'd come home and go through my mother's stuff and put on her stockings and make a flapper's hat with a paper bag. The race was always against the clock: my parents would leave and I'd see how much stuff I could put on before they came back home.

I was never really in the closet. But at the end of my high school years I really came out. I started wearing high heels and women's clothing and I had a dress tucked into my pants. The day before I graduated I opened my jacket, and the dress fell down. Then I took off my shoes and put on high heels. Everyone was taking Quaaludes and acid and they were flipped out. They couldn't believe it. One other seminal experience in Catholic school involved a Franciscan brother who I was very intimate with. We never had sex. We were about to once but he stopped it. He eventually left the brotherhood and became [long pause, innocently] a porno star. My formal education was short-lived after that. The second year in college I dropped out, becoming a hippie freak going to parties and love-ins. It was 1971, glam rock days. I joined a group called the Groundlings: Phil Hartmann and Lorraine Newman of Saturday Night Live were from the Groundlings. So was Pee-Wee Herman and Elvira. I was in a rock band called The Capital. It was a wild old time, all right. A lot of people got lost during the Sixties and Seventies. To do drag and performance you have to be cen-

I WAS NEVER REALLY IN THE CLOSET

tered. You have to know who you are. You are using so much of the culture as a resource for visuals that if you don't have a strong sense of identity you'll lose your way. Lots of people—the Jackie Curtis's—burnt themselves out.

Actually, I never thought of it as drag. I was just always into wigs and heels and dressing up. Dress-up changes to drag with recognition. I've always been doing it but the recognition changes it. Suddenly, you find all this power related to it. People's responses are dramatic; they're overwhelmed. All at once, this word "drag" starts coming at you: Drag...drag...drag. RuPaul said you're born naked and everything you put on after that is drag. A business suit is drag—as much as a dress or a clown's outfit. Whatever you're wearing, that's your drag for the day. I guess it has other meanings: drag, drag queen, drag race...who knows...just drag bitch [laughs]. Drag led to my involvement with what I call "transformations." With Ann Magnuson I'd do these shows and turn into completely different characters: devils and mermaids, dragons and monsters. Just playing with myself, visually. When I first came to New York I went to a party with Kenny Scharf and Ann Magnuson, dressed up in this outfit with great big bazoongas and heavy dark makeup. They asked who I was and I noticed a book on the shelf by the Marquis de Sade, *Justine.* So I said, "Hi, my name is Justine." And that's how the character was born.

My idea with Justine was to be a superwoman. I started feeling what a woman might go through. How men might try to take advantage of you just because you were wearing certain clothing—the pinching and the comments—so I created Justine so that she would fight for a woman's rights. Women meet me and say, "I wish I was like Justine." Because Justine has men coming up to her saying, "Oh baby," and she pushes them away, "Get out of here!" Justine also becomes a heavy sex thing. Woman are always touching the breasts. They touch you like you're a deity. Justine is a 42-D, with twenty-five-inch waist, forty-eight-inch hips, standing about 6'2" and ready to shoot anyone down. That's the power of Justine. My whole body goes into contortions to become Justine. But when I do, I don't think like Joey any more. And if Justine was sitting here, it would be a whole different interview.

What are Justine's breasts made out of? Love! Anyway, I'm not going to tell you my trade secrets. Though I can't reveal that they're very realistic and life-like. In London, I told people they cost $5,000 each and they all said, "well worth it, love." It's all in the cut and the construction. It's also in the body language. Other queens try, but they don't have a rhythm to their bodies. When they are on my body they're my tits. If they are on the floor you can kick them, but when they're on my body they're mine. Justine is a transatlantic transsexual busted in Paris. It's true! Once I was picked up by the French police. The police couldn't believe Justine. But most people give her respect, even open doors for Justine—or she busts them down. Justine's not nasty, she's not vicious; she's just a fun-loving kind of girl. Justine gets people going.

After Justine was "born," I started singing like Billie Holiday. Just for fun, not as a performance. I listened to Billie Holiday records as a kid and I loved the texture and feeling that came out of her voice. I would just sing along with her, the way she sang along with Louis Armstrong or Bessie Smith. My favorite Billie Holiday is "God Bless the Child," or "Good Morning Heartbreak." I kept singing and singing until the same sound came out of me. But people kept saying, do that in drag. I didn't think I could do it. But one day I saw a picture on the cover of *Lady in Satin*. She had her hair pulled back in a simple ponytail and a sort of painted forehead. So I decided to do a visual homage to Lady Day. There's a sensibility in the voice, mine and Billie's, that people like to hear. I could never have been doing this show ten years ago. It wasn't ripe yet. So you could call me a well-seasoned, strange fruit.

Oh, but to go back to my life, when I came to New York, I came with Kim, the editor of *Paper* magazine. She had just graduated from Cal Arts and she packed up her truck, and we went shoplifting, oops, I mean shopping, across America. We had a great time. I was wearing a khaki jungle jacket and kohl in my eyes, which was already freaking people out. The trip

took two weeks. When I saw New York I was thrilled. My dream was to become a big star and to meet Andy Warhol and just be famous. And all my dreams came true. I hung out with Andy Warhol, worked with my favorite stars like David Bowie on *Saturday Night Live* and toured all over Europe.

After the Bowie tour I went to Ibiza to do a show there, two days after James Brown had been there. They said, "You'd better be good or we'll throw your ass out." I thought to myself: "If I get over with this then I know this is what I'm supposed to be doing for life. If this thing is a flop then I'm going to just stop." I did a show that represented the decadence of New York City, taking all the bad parts but twisting it around to make it fun. I had lots of clothes on and a G-string and it was sort of a strip show, and I had a giant dildo which I would pretend to sit on while singing "Devil With a Blue Dress." I would bring girls on stage and tear their panties off and try to bite their pussies. I also tried to bite guys' asses. They went wild and the owners paid me lots of money and told me I was the star of Ibiza. That was in 1987. Then I had a show called Mermaids on Heroin. There were all these people in mermaid costumes and I was the kind mermaid. It was an anti-pollution statement. Once a month at Danceteria there would be these shows. The B-52's were there and Cindy Lauper and others.

This was during the Ziggy Stardust period and the whole androgyny thing. My dream was to sing with Bowie, always that song "*TVC-15*." And when we worked together he said, "I wish I had met you earlier." Then I got involved in the Hip-Hop scene, when Madonna was breaking into the charts. So we went on tour, Madonna and Mann Parish and *moi*. We worked in black clubs and Puerto Rican clubs and we started that whole woo-woo-woo that you see on *The Arsenio Hall Show*.

On Mann's record there was a dog barking. So whenever

JOEY ARIAS

he came out the announcer would say: "Ladies and Gentlemen, Mann Parish." And the crowd would go woo-woo-woo. That's where 'doing the dog bark' started. Then they threw me out of the group (we had our differences). So I hooked up with Ann Magnuson, who said, "Fuck all those people. Why should you work to make them look good? Do it yourself." So we teamed up—she was doing her thing already anyway. She said: "Why don't you be Andy Warhol and I'll be Edie Sedgewick!" We created the Andy & Edie Show, then the Dolly & Guy Show and the Charles Manson & Squeaky Show. We did them at clubs and in videos and public access shows. Then some people contacted me and asked me to be on the cover of a magazine called *Drag 88*. They offered me $500 so I pulled Justine out and posed for the picture. A lot of people saw the magazine—it became a calendar—and one thing led to another. First Justine was coming out once a month, then once a week, and then almost every day. When I started doing the drag full-time she said: "What happened to you, Joey?" I guess Justine is it for the Nineties.

It still puzzles me. Drag really revived in the late Eighties—though drag has been around, it was always an underground scene. It was always in dark places with no humor to it. It was more about sex and perversion—not about fun and color and excitement and inventing characters. It didn't have the notoriety. The scene in the Eighties was depressed because of AIDS, and there were only these huge impersonal clubs and no sense of community. Then people like Suzanne Bartsch started doing little clubs and saying sex was all right. Now it's become an art form. It's part of being proud of who you are. In a way, being gay is one of the last taboos and drag is a way to embrace it and have fun with it. By the time the film *Paris Is Burning* came out, drag parties and club events were going strong.

My contribution to all this? I brought drag and performance together. I was always a singer first. In New York everything has a title. We were doing these kooky shows in kooky places so we became "performance artists." Now, drag is absolutely everywhere: England, Los Angeles, San Francisco, Berlin, Paris. Tons in Japan. In Paris, the queens are all wearing

Balenciaga gowns, all done up in their silicone tits and their fixed noses. But there's a certain energy about the queens in New York, in the way they put themselves together. (There are so many makeup tips!) Other places I've been, queens have their beards showing through and their makeup is all blue and they want to know how we New York girls do it all.

But it's definitely not about trying to be a woman. Hey, I like my penis! I like that penis! There are transsexuals, transvestites, female illusionists, crossdressers, and perverts, too. Look at Michael Jackson: now that's a perverted drag. And who knows—Tonya Harding might be a drag from Akron, Ohio! There are straight guys who do drag, too. Years ago my father put on my mother's high heels to walk around the house. Look, everyone does a little drag—but mostly in the closet.

My family are great about it now. When I did the Billie Holiday show in Los Angeles, Madonna was there, and other celebrities, and my dad came. And I realized this was it—the big reality check. Here I was, obviously gay, and in a dress and I said: "Here I am, Dad. It's how I pay the rent." He came up after the show and wanted to know when I was going to get married. But I told him, "I'm not a breeder, it's not my calling."

I had a brother who died of cancer; I also have a sister, and two younger brothers. They are all straight. One brother's a doctor and one's a construction worker. My sister is a mother and works in a hospital. They've come to the show and they love it. They're real dudes and they think it's cool. My mother died a few years ago; I was very close to her.

Where's drag going? Now it's fashionable so it's out of fashion. By the time this book comes out it'll be back in again. People are always looking for the next thing. For me it's an art and true art lasts forever. But I'm the art, I'm the canvas. I'll just keep doing what I'm doing. I don't know what I'll metamorphose into when tomorrow comes.

People know that there's a little bit of a man and woman in everybody. Most people don't know how much or who they are. It's about your heart beating a certain way. Now drags are seen as the shaman priests of the gay world. I see drag as the punk of the Nineties. It's out to break barriers. What punk did for the Seventies, drag will do for the Nineties.

Now my life is like a three-ring circus. Here I am, mixing straight and gay and this whole new concept with the Cirque du Soleil. It has music, drag, and androgyny. I'm the ringmaster and you can't tell if I'm a man or a woman. I have two drag back-up singers. The band seems straight, and they are, but after me and the drags you can't be sure. In fact, my fantasy is my life. Whatever I think about I make come true. Here I am in my Beaujolais years doing what I did as a kid but getting paid for it. It's wonderful.

What's Joey's message to the world? Be strong, be centered, be healthy, love, shine a light and don't judge people. Be open. Care for your brother. Be open to experiences in life. Let your mind travel. Live your fantasies and dreams. Let dreams come true. That's my message. And what would I say to people who are a little scared? [Yelling] Fuck off!

FUCK OFF

# MATHU AND ZALDY

*MATHU ANDERSON AND ZALDY GOCO ARE TWO THAT ARE ONE. TRANSCENDING FASHION AND DRAG ITSELF TO PERFORM THEIR LIVING, BREATHING CREATIONS OF SELF-STYLING, THEIR UNIQUE PERFORMANCE ART HAS BEEN IMMORTALIZED BY MANY OF THE GREAT NAMES IN FASHION PHOTOGRAPHY, INCLUDING MEISEL, WATSON, ELGORT, AND SCAVULLO. NOW THEY ARE IMAGE MAKERS IN THEIR OWN RIGHT, WORKING FOR DONNA KARAN, SHISEIDO, AND FELLOW ENTERTAINER RUPAUL. WE INTERVIEWED THEM, CLAD IN SILK PAJAMAS, OVER MORNING COFFEE IN THEIR CHELSEA HOTEL LOFT.*

**M.** The ideal woman today? No one can attain that. The amount of makeup and the retouching involved creates a freak of nature six feet tall with oversized lips. It's a big lie.

**Z.** But if you met some of those models without the makeup and the airbrushing and saw the acned skin, the bags, the wrinkles! The illusion, believe me, is the real business.

**M.** We are a society that works purely on visuals; the other senses are secondary. Ergo, being beautiful is a great way to get things. That said, beauty and intelligence don't come together in the same package very often. Beauty is what's deemed attractive by the consensus of opinion.

**Z.** But we've redefined the criteria for ourselves. We want to look like men. But men in full tie and a corset. And it's still drag.

**M.** Wanting to look like a man is just as big a joke as wanting to look like a woman. It's just another set of rules to play with. Gender's still the game.

Interview

**Z.** Gender's never really been the problem.

**M.** Though body adornment (which drag is part of) will always be an important part of human experience, drag is a process of reaching inside. Anything that makes people move outside their own compartment is important. That said, the drag world feels sometimes like it's not a real world, but a bubble. Still, it is a defining process. People look at queens and say they are frivolous. Part of my family is like that towards gays in general—with the attitude that they should be taken out and shot, that it's not Christian. But the gay backlash toward drag is what's scary, conservative gays who feel drag is dragging down the gay cause. See a therapist! Have sex more often! Get a better diet! And get over it! The gay backlash toward drag became apparent to me when we did an event one night at the Rainbow Room. Powerful gay political figures were there and there was this animosity: "Get thee back from whence thou came." Look, gay feminine/masculine politics are sad. Sure, everyone's angry. But anger isn't going to solve anything. Let me work on the pride of being alive and human before I work on the (in a Scottish accent) "I'm gay and pruud" role-playing thing. We've just chosen to explain our role-playing in a more visible, out-there sort of way. I don't hold with the gay movement because it's so militant and boisterous. You're not going to win a war by screaming and jumping up and down. It's not very P.C. I know, but if you just listened to everything everyone said, you'd just sit in a corner facing a wall and saying, "I can't, I can't." Everything you say is construed as a political act anyway, so you'll always please some and offend others. Even in fashion you can't believe how odd these forward-

thinking, trend-minded people are–*weird.*

**Z.** People do respond to us, in the strongest way possible. People respect the talent behind the look—they're looking at a quality piece of work here. It is unique and hasn't followed anyone. Though we pay homage to many who've gone before, we've always been experimental in the way we look—in fabrics, body shapes, and in trying different ways to push it.

**M.** Things that arise out of a scribble, a doodle, a moment are all opportunities for us to stretch the envelope. Over the years Zaldy and I have had screaming arguments, but when it works, I feel I have found a soul mate, a part of me I don't have, a total partner in creating.

**Z.** When did we meet? After I came to New York from California, in 1985.

**M.** I wanted to stop being a square peg in a round hole in Australia so I took my makeup book around and tried to get work. I'm still a makeup artist (but somewhat more successful now). I do magazine work: *Vogue, Town and Country,* and advertising, too. I started when I was twenty, in college—when I wanted to be a fashion designer. Of course at twelve I wanted to work for Disney as an animator, and at sixteen I wanted to be an illustrator *a la* Frank Frazetta. But this was at Sydney College of Arts; I ended up with a B.A. in Fashion and Textile Design. I would do makeup for others' pictures—witness the experiments on my younger sisters, trying horrible things with Maybelline. After five years of making mistakes in public, I got a reasonable reputation as being somewhat wacky and was told I should go to Europe. I got to New York and stopped. It

# GENDER'S NEVER BEEN THE PROBLEM.

was a long, hard crawl to get my work to the point it is now. Now I am considered one of New York's top makeup artists—for whatever that's worth. My reputation is still left of center and the drag queen work has given me a certain notoriety, even more of a license to be kooky. This started when I met Zaldy, at the end of '89. I was actually married, then. My wife is a lovely girl (I mean *woman*. Sorry darling, that I called you a girl!) I met her when I was seventeen. She started working her way up in magazines as a very talented writer and landed a job starting *Sassy* magazine. She went to New York and I went with her. I don't think I would have done it alone at that point.

**Z.**Mathu and I actually met later, on a Josef Astor photo shoot—but he was still married then. I was posing and Mathu was there and I said, "Do you want to go out for a drink," and he said, "No, I have to go home to my wife." Which left me very puzzled and I didn't see him for months and months after that, until our first magical night at the Copacabana, dancing to "Never Can Say Goodbye," and that's what it's been like....

**M.**So who are we? What was the genesis of Matthew's style? I asked my mother "Was I good at drawing when I was young?" "No, darling," she said, "you didn't seem to exhibit any talent whatsoever." I spent a lot of time alone as a child, and the combination of being very shy and somewhat spacy made people think I was mentally retarded. Books were an early source of inspiration. I had a favorite set on fairies, giants, mermaids, princesses, and dragons, different stories from different countries of the world, with wonderfully fine pen and ink illustrations—very detailed. Then, too, I was always a macabre child, interested in monsters and all kinds of creepy-crawlies. I was so horrendously shy I don't think I spoke more than four words a day: "please," "thanks" and "may I." My two sisters are seven years younger, so I spent a lot of time alone drawing, too, making dollies for myself with my colored markers.

I grew up in Hornsby, on a plot of land in a nice, big, semi-rural area which my grandfather had bought and built the house himself. My father never quite lived up to him. I didn't get along with my father, who would have liked a son more rough and tumble, someone who would get under the lawnmower with him and pull it to pieces. (Fortunately, my brother came along and provided him with that outlet.) No matter how much my father wanted to like me and no matter how much I tried to have him like me we just didn't do it for each other. He had a very unfortunate accident when I was five, receiving a head injury that made him fly off the handle about anything. I spent most of my time consequently paralyzed with fear. The biggest treat was when Dad wasn't home. I can't say I enjoyed being a child. I can only remember "fairy," "pansy." They should have just rechristened me at that point—it would have been easier.

By high school at an all-boys school, I found that the best way to stave off attacks was to get interested in females. So I developed a fascination with fantasy comic art, the barbarian variety, full of two-headed lizards snaking around nubile women with big hair, a few chains, and pasties. I had a very camp sensibility and liked the exaggeration of cartoons, anything that was funny and smacked of unreality; things that didn't tie into the everyday. It had a violent side: Daffy Duck, all the Warner stuff, and Bugs Bunny. I also loved Japanese cartoons, like Generation X, Astro Boy, or Planet of the Planet and Rocky, Bullwinkle, and Fractured Fairy Tales were genius. My favorite was the vaguely naughty Travel Guides, with the syrupy announcer: "Here's a lizard sunning on a rock. Lizards shed their skin." Then the lizard jumps up, rips his zips—and there's this naked female body underneath, with a lizard's tail. I've never been interested in drawing men, though—always big, oversized females. Hell, I married one. My wife looks like a beautiful Flemish madonna, with huge blue eyes and strong nose and a beautiful rosebud mouth. Not classical but an extremely beautiful woman.

**Z.**My mother's Filipino and Spanish and my father is Filipino and Chinese. I was actually born and raised in Connecticut, in a very conservative family. They are all doctors, married to doctors, and sons and daughters of doctors. I don't know why

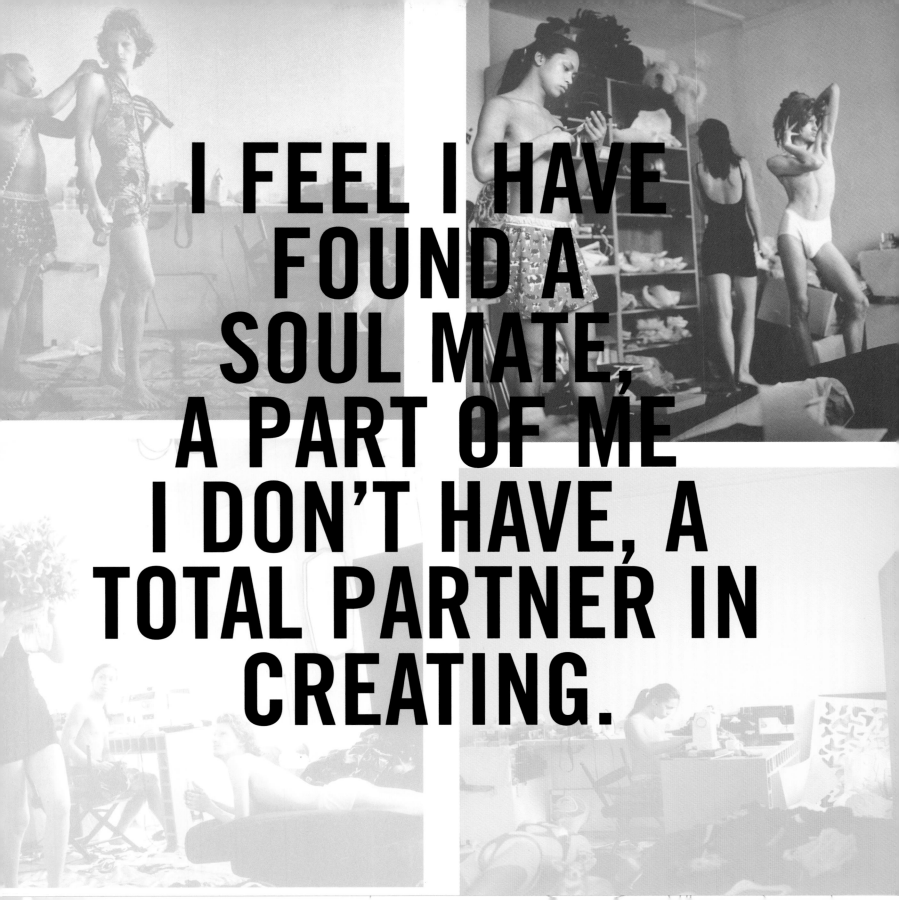

I FEEL I HAVE FOUND A SOUL MATE, A PART OF ME I DON'T HAVE, A TOTAL PARTNER IN CREATING.

*Hardly your standard disco diva, Lypsinka (born John Eperson in Jackson, Mississippi) is a master of a thousand voices, all taken from her vast curatorial collection of old movie dialogue and record albums. Lypsinka's extraordinary range has raised the venerable drag tradition to a new high as an art form. We caught up with her in England, where her cabaret act is packing theaters, as it has since the moment she put lips to a microphone.*

**Interview**

THE HISTORY OF DRAG, THE KIND OF PERFORMANCE CALLED PANTOMIME, IS AN OLD TRADITION. BUT WHAT *I* DO IS A LITTLE MORE SUBVERSIVE THAN THAT. WHAT I DO IS REALLY A COMMENT ON DRAG PERFORMANCE. CALL IT POSTMODERNIST, I GUESS—THOUGH IRONICALLY. I STARTED DOING THIS SELF-CRITIQUE WITHOUT EVEN KNOWING WHAT THE TERM MEANT. I INTENDED THAT THE NAME LYPSINKA BE SELF-REFLECTIVE BUT AT THE SAME TIME I DIDN'T KNOW *WHY*. LADY BUNNY WAS ONCE ASKED, "COULD WHAT YOU DO BE CALLED *PASTICHE*?" AND BUNNY SAID, "I GUESS, IF I KNEW WHAT IT MEANT!"

I HAVE A DEGREE IN MUSIC FROM A TINY PRESBYTERIAN COLLEGE CALLED BELLE HAVEN. IT WAS IN A BEAUTIFUL NEIGHBORHOOD IN JACKSON, NEAR THE HOME OF EUDORA WELTY. THE WORLD THAT SHE WROTE ABOUT IS THE WORLD I GREW UP IN: MODERN GOTHIC, SOUTHERN ECCENTRIC, ALMOST SOUTHERN GROTESQUE ATMOSPHERE. VERY DEEP SOUTH—THE WEATHER IS VERY HUMID, THE FLORA AND FAUNA VERY THICK. VERY BEAUTIFUL, BUT VERY TWISTED. I'M GLAD I GOT OUT.

FOR ME DRAG BEGAN BY GETTING ATTENTION FROM MY FAMILY BY LIP-SYNCHING TO FEMALE RECORDS. OF COURSE, I HAD MY SISTERS TO COMPETE WITH. WHEN I GOT THAT ATTENTION, IT WAS LIKE BEING A PAVLOV DOG—IT GAVE ME SOMETHING TO FEED OFF, APPEALED TO THE SHOWBIZ PERSON

inside of me, who exists "God only knows how". Why do people get bit by the showbiz bug? A mystery—no one else in my family has any interest in it. And it's a big family full of people doing the bunny hop. My mother's side is from Mississippi and my father's from Louisiana. My oldest sister loved entertaining my other sister and me. She would put on puppet shows and bring Barbra Streisand and Beatles records home. I was introduced to a whole pop scene by her.

My parents liked going to movies also. I remember seeing *Psycho* at a drive-in when I was a very young kid. My mother was very upset, she just thanked the Lord that we all fell asleep before it got to the murder scene. I have vivid, vivid memories of going to see *Marnie*, absolutely my favorite, as well as going to see *How The West Was Won* in Cinerama. I had a totally visceral experience seeing Ann Margret in *Bye Bye Birdie,* specifically the opening scene when she sings the title song, and then later on when she sings "Lotta Living to Do," which is a very sexy number. 'Course, I didn't know from sex, but subliminally it was appealing.

There is also home movie footage of me deflecting attention from my sister by going into this little storehouse we had (we called it the playhouse) and putting on a dress and coming out and parading around in it. As the movie rolls, you can see my mother smiling at me approvingly. She's got a badminton racket in her hand; totally 1950s. Then my father's first cousin finds a dress, and *he* starts prancing around. But *I* started the trend, you see; it's all there on film. I have always thought that what I do now is what I did as a kid. It's a totally childhood thing to lip-synch.

I had no outlet as a boy, except to play the piano, which is what I did all the way through school, though I was also in the high school band, playing the saxophone. Frankly, I was talented as a pianist. But I often froze in performance—I never felt free playing in front of people, though I put myself through the trauma year after year. When I got to college I auditioned for the annual musical. It was an old Carol Burnett vehicle (the one that made her a star), called *Once Upon a Mattress.* My

character's name was Sir Studly, which was perverse of the director to do because I was a flaming queen. I didn't know it, but I was. I was very effeminate and confused, scared and frightened. The princess and the pea is the story and the girl who was my partner was the princess. There is a number in the show called "The Spanish Panic" and as we presented it, the audience howled and howled with laughter. I didn't know it was supposed to be funny. But I realized you could make a complete fool of yourself and instead of having the audience laugh at you, have them laugh with you. So that's what I did. The irony is, I was totally obsessed with the TV performances of Carol Burnett, and here I was doing the show that made her famous. The next night it was an even bigger hit—I developed this comic ability overnight. That reaction from the audience was totally addictive. It represented the kind of relief that I had wanted as a pianist, but never found playing classical music.

I continued to do other musicals, but I didn't have the nerve to tell my family that I really didn't want to play the piano. I wanted to be a movie star; I wanted to be an *actor.* The world of classical music is very competitive, probably much more competitive than trashy show business. But playing the piano is much more practical—you can always teach, or accompany singers, or accompany ballet. My mother kept telling me that she wanted me to get a teacher's license; I kept saying I didn't have any intention of teaching, I was going to make a living at this one way or another.

So I went back to Mississippi and worked at a ballet company playing the piano. The film *The Turning Point* had come out, which sparked a nationwide interest in dance. I got caught up in that even though I was twenty-two, too old to become a real dancer, certainly a real ballet dancer. During that year I saw Gelsey Kirkland twice on television—absolutely brilliant. I can't praise this woman enough; the spark and the magic that she had in her heyday! I was already laying my plans to go back to New York. So I moved there in 1978 and lived in a transient hotel and started working as a pianist for the ABT school. In the meantime I was still looking into real

KODAK TXP 6049

52

KODAK TXP 6049

show business, but I was so intimidated by it; I didn't have the faintest idea of how to break in.

New York suddenly opened up this whole world where I realized that my interests were really much more esoteric than what mainstream show business was offering. I consciously said to myself "Just wait—your niche will find you!" New York in 1978 was an unbelievable haven for films. Museums, repertory theaters and all kinds of little nooks and crannies showed movies then. *The Village Voice* would print all those weird places where you could go see arcane things like *Mary Sings* at the Collective for Living Cinema on White Street. Among them, there was this little place called Club 57 on St. Marks Place, showing *Beyond the Valley of the Dolls*. The credits started rolling, and the people there, all these kids my age, were going absolutely insane. The name Edie Williams flashed on the screen—I didn't know who the hell Edie Williams was, but everyone else did! I thought to myself "Something is going on here—and it's not about Edie Williams; it's about the *reaction* to her." I thought, "You have found your niche."

Looking back, twenty-three doesn't seem that young. But you have to remember I was such a green kid from Mississippi. I was emotionally very young; I hadn't lived. Twenty-three-year-olds now, who grow up in New York, have lived lifetimes. I asked Ann Magnuson, who was the manager of Club 57, if I could become a member. The hipper-than-thou attitude of the place was so thick you could cut it with a knife. While completely intimidated by Ann and all the other people, I was still determined to go as often as possible because the movies they showed were so outrageous. The next film was *Faster Pussy Cat Kill Kill* (Russ Meyer also).

After many movies, I started performing at the club. My first effort was a mock Lawrence Welk show. Kenny Scharf was Lawrence Welk. I was Joanne Castle, who was the ragtime piano player on the Lawrence Welk show. I also played the piano for the Lennon sisters (Ann was one of the Lennon sisters). What we were doing was completely a mockery of show business. We thought we were making wonderful jokes.

I DON'T THINK I HAVE EVER REALLY INVENTED MYSELF, WHAT I DO IS FIND MYSELF.

Singing a medley of "Don't Cry for Me Argentina," "What I did for Love" and "Tomorrow" from *Annie*. That act, or a show that John Sex pulled together called *Acts of Live Art*, was the first time I ever performed in drag. But the summer of 1979 was the first time I ever lip-lip-lip-synched in public. John and Kenny and Anne, and Keith Haring were around, and Joey Arias, and a little later Holly Woodlawn got involved. Mark Shaman and Mark Whitman came after I pulled out (Mark was nominated for an Academy Award for his song in *Sleepless in Seattle*.) Every night there was something different. God only knows how Ann had the energy. But back then we all had a *lot* of energy.

Every Tuesday was the monster movie club, and I went to just all of them. Some nights it would be packed. It would be a fire trap—the cigarette smoke was even thicker than the hipper-than-thou attitude. And when that place finally closed, the Pyramid Club opened. The Pyramid was intended (by Bobby Bradly who started it) to be a cross between the Anvil and Club 57. I pulled out because I got a full-time job with the ABT, working with Natalia Markarova as her own private pianist, going on the road and traveling everywhere with them, seeing the world. After a while I grew disillusioned. John Sex encouraged me to start performing again and in 1982 I thought of the name Lypsinka.

AIDS had a lot to do with that decision. When AIDS came along I said to myself, "Well, you can't have sex anymore, might as well have a career." By 1985 it became apparent to me that the character Lypsinka was becoming more popular in the East Village. I produced a show at the Pyramid called *Ballet of the Dolls*, a parody of the ballet world and *Valley of the Dolls*. It played six performances, sold out every night. And I thought, "Well, you really do have *something* here." I continued to per-

form as Lypsinka, and in 1986 the Pyramid said "Do another show." So I wrote *Dial M for Model*, inspired by the Millie the Model comic books, and that, too, was very successful and hooked me into La Mama, where we did it in 1987. Then I did my first performance as Lypsinka at La Mama, the first time ever in front of a seated crowd. When I arrived that night, they said "It's sold out." I was completely surprised. In January 1988, we revived *Ballet of the Dolls* at La Mama, and it sold out.

In spring 1988 I decided to do Lypsinka as a theatrical thing for five performances—sold out. Charles Bush came to the show and persuaded his roommate, who was the director of *Vampire Lesbians of Sodom,* to come see the show. They asked if I would do a late-night show after *Vampire Lesbians*—sold out. Joan Rivers came to see it. Elton John came. Then another theater optioned it, and in November of 1988 we reopened it, and it ran until September of 1989. I'm totally exhausted to even think that I did that for a year, but I did. It was an amazing year for me, a textbook year, where I learned a lot, got a lot of publicity. I said "This is ridiculous," made a whole new show and staged it myself and took it to San Francisco where it (guess what), sold out, and then went to Los Angeles. I keep saying "sold out" but it's true! It did! And it's something to be proud of.

In L.A. the stars started coming out to see me (the whole thing was very hot at the time): Madonna, Sandra Bernhard, Bette Midler. I went back to San Francisco and did my show again. The people in L.A. brought potential investors to the show, and got the money to bring me back to L.A. Madonna was one of the investors, which didn't hurt publicity. It all comes full circle. One night Carol Burnett showed up, laughing her head off, and came backstage and hugged me; that was an

# PEOPLE WANT GLAMOUR

amazing thing for me. All the cast of *Golden Girls*, except Betty White, came. David Bowie was there, and even people like Faye Dunaway knew who the hell I was. I am completely starstruck, so this was very heady stuff for me. It's a miracle. If this had all happened to me ten years earlier I probably would have been a nightmare to deal with, but I'm not at all jaded. Since it happened rather late in my life, it was easier to handle.

I don't think I have ever really invented myself, what I do is find myself. I have been (if you want to get into this) in psychotherapy since 1990. What I realized is that when I was about fourteen, I (like many other people, especially many gay men) put this outer layer of charm and wit and sophistication (which is really pseudo-sophistication) around myself, in order to get through what I had to get through, which was being a complete outcast in a small southern town.

To want to play the piano, to read books, to do all the things that boys aren't supposed to do, was a tough thing. And it took psychoanalysis for me to wade through all those layers of shit. I have been terribly, terribly depressed in my lifetime. It is a pattern I picked up from my father. I am not blaming him—he couldn't help it—I think he got it from his mother. And I am not sure that any parents would have been any more understanding of me as a little weird kid,

even if my older sister had not died. When that happened, my other sister also retreated into depression. But, now she has come through it, and we have a great relationship. When finally my father came to New York a year ago, and saw my performance, saw New York, saw my life and saw that I had turned myself into something, all by myself, he said a very beautiful thing to me, a very sensitive thing. I realized that I finally had his approval. As far as having a complete understanding from my family, that's never going to happen, and I realize that.

Now I have a film to look forward to called *Witch Hunt*, where I play the Madam of a high-class whorehouse, who changes the girls' faces and bodies to please the clients. As much as I love performing live, it is totally exhausting, especially when it means traveling around. I can't figure out why Paul Schrader wants to make this movie but he said they want it to be "hip," which is one of the reasons he wanted me. It amuses me that I am the arbiter of hip. I, who would rather stay home than do anything!

My most recent last show in New York competed with two huge musicals, *Angels in America* and *Kiss of the Spider Woman*, and I was also coming on the heels of my own performance. Then Bunny, very cruel and funny, said, "If you'd called your show Lypsinka has AIDS it would have succeeded."

The songs I am doing right now? The first is special material, originally written for Gizelle McKenzie's nightclub act at the Waldorf Astoria in the Fifties; it's called "An Opening Song." Some of the other songs are "To Be a Performer" from a musical called *Little Me* (the singer I'm using is Katrina Valente). There is a lot of Dolores Gray—she is pretty much the Lypsinka prototype—singing "There Will Be Some Changes Made" and "Around the World." There is Mimi Hines singing "I'm the Greatest Star," Lauren Bacall singing "I'm Alive," a song from *Applause*, and a bit of Judy Squires (who's a sort of fifth-rate Judy Garland type here in England) singing "I Gotta Be Me." There is a crazy recording of "Mame" by Fay McKay, (who no one's ever heard of except for me and a handful of other people). Then there is Connie Francis singing "Once in a Lifetime" and Libby Morris singing "Tea for Two." I don't change my performance for England, but I do see that they are no longer interested in slapstick. My show was tried and true in the United States. But the more emotional stuff seems to be appealing to the English.

I have this theory about the why of drag, probably one you haven't heard. Bunny's theory is that people want glamour, and the female stars aren't giving it. It's a good theory, kind of true. Other people have theories that come out of the gay movement or out of the women's movement, because due to those movements gender has become less important. What I saw happening in the East Village was that the whole hot-bed of the art movement of the Eighties wasn't just art: it was fashion, it was performance, it was visual art, it was music, it was how people were looking at pop culture of the past, the far past, the recent past. That was an attitude slowly trickled down to the mainstream. Call it New Wave, call it East Village, call it Eighties, whatever. When we used to go to Club 57 there would be whole nights of watching Warner Bros. cartoons, or sitcoms from the early Sixties, like *The Donna Reed Show, The Patty Duke Show*. Girls from Club 57 like Ann and Susan Haniford Rose were all wearing leopard skin as a joke. Now *The New York Times* fashion pages are all about leopard skin. There are whole TV stations devoted to cartoons, devoted to Donna Reed and Dick Van Dyke. We saw the *Flintstones* coming, along with all of "cartoon style." Drag is just the last stronghold of the East Village thing. The reason it's the last one is because it threatens peoples' sexuality (the *Flintstones* doesn't). People are saying drag is mainstream now. I don't think it really is, it's not really mom and pop. There is no drag TV station. RuPaul's album, for all the publicity, was not that big a success. *Paris Is Burning,* for all its celebrity, made little money. Sure, there is *The Crying Game* and there is *Mrs. Doubtfire,* but while I didn't see *The Crying Game, Mrs. Doubtfire* is very safe, and *not* about being sexy.

The rest of drag is more self-conscious now. A critic got it right on the money  (and no one else ever has before) saying that what I was doing was "a celebration of female stardom and at the same time a critique of show business iconography." It took me years until I figured out what it meant. Drag is now elevated to a completely abstract concept.

Quentin Crisp as Queen Elizabeth in the film *Orlando*.

# QUENTIN
# CRISP

Interview

*Mr. Crisp joined us for lunch sporting a violet fedora and matching cravat, complete with walking stick. He looked resplendent. Rumored to be about eighty-six years of age, he gained international fame in 1976 when the dramatization of his autobiography,* The Naked Civil Servant, *was televised both in his native Great Britain and here in America. Since then he has resided in New York and enjoys a successful career as a famous wit, writer, and lecturer. He also authored* How to Go to the Movies, How to Become a Virgin, Manners from Heaven (*a book of etiquette*) *and* Quentin Crisp's Book of Quotations.

THE NAKED CIVIL SERVANT CAUSED A GREAT STIR IN ENGLAND. IN FACT, A MS. BANKS SMITH, A TELEVISION CRITIC IN ENGLAND, SAID IT "JUSTIFIED THE EXISTENCE OF TELEVISION." I WASN'T KNOWN BEFORE THAT—I LIVED IN OBSCURITY. I WAS, OF COURSE, KNOWN, THAT IS TO SAY, REMEMBERED, WHEN YOU SAW ME. BECAUSE WHAT THE NAKED CIVIL SERVANT DOESN'T SHOW YOU IS THE CROWDS THAT FOLLOWED ME. AND THE POLICEMEN WOULD COME AND PUSH THEIR WAY THROUGH AND WOULD SAY, "OH, IT'S YOU AGAIN," AND MOVE THE PEOPLE ON. MAVIS NICOLSON, AN INTERVIEWER ON ENGLISH TELEVISION, SHOWED THE NAKED CIVIL SERVANT TO A POLICEMAN, WHO SAID "CAN'T BE TRUE—HE'D'VE BEEN ARRESTED ON THE FIRST DAY." YOU SEE, TO THE LAW, A MAN MUST NOT DRESS AS A WOMAN BECAUSE HE MIGHT GET INTO SITUATIONS THAT ARE unallowed, like going into a women's lavatory. If you managed to establish an alibi somewhere, well and good, but without it you were arrested. If you had been walking on the street you had only to stop and talk to someone and you were arrested. The prejudice was considerable. For in London if you are conspicuously effeminate you are in danger. All the time.

I lived in London all my life, except when I was a child. I wore makeup by the time I was twenty, but very little at first. I never wore foundation. I wore face powder—which I wear now. I wore entinimin rouge, which I rather think was lipstick. I wore eyeshadow and I wore mascara. It absolutely flummoxed people. Makeup is like a drug—I can take a dose now that would kill anyone just starting out. But I wore more, more—till my eyebrows were in single file; my eyelashes were out to here; my fingernails were so long that there was more of the nail than the finger. It was a gradual process, to be sure. One comes to have a vision of oneself in the world. And I suppose I do—I wish everyone did. Because the whole point of your appearance is that it cuts away the deadwood of human relationships. It means you don't have to put up with any generalizations; nobody talks to me about the weather!

For me, the movies were the genesis of drag. All movies were built on the idea that it might be possible to rule the world through the skillful use of cosmetics. Before there were American movies there were silent movies. I thought them beautiful. And when I saw America for the first time I thought, "It's more like the movies than I ever dreamed!" As I said to Roddy McDowall (who came to New York to photograph me), "Go to see the silent films, the silent eyes, because they are absurd but they are also beautiful." In the silent film period, nearly all the great beauties played vamps (the word has disappeared now) and those roles started as ideas in somebody's head. Garbo was an idea in Maurice Stiller's head. Dietrich was an idea in Von Sternberg's head. But Dietrich was more worldly than the others and even when Von Sternberg was gone she could still stand on any set and feel the light on her face and that's where she directed them to photograph her.

One marvelous film star, Miss Helm, was invented by Fritz Lang when he filled in the space between her eyes with string and sealing wax. And when he photographed her, then she knew who she was—and could do it forever. She was the subject of the first science fiction movie ever made; it's called *Metropolis*. It has a mad scientist in the laboratory, pipes, steam, discs, dials, and in this amazing room they make an artificial Miss Helm. Because Miss Helm is a good woman (that's to say her hair in front is untidy) the artificial Miss Helm is given straight hair. With a rather glib use of electricity they construct her. And the only difference between the real and artificial Miss Helm is that the artificial one has no soul and one eye never shuts. It's absurd, but absolutely wonderful.

I thought I could rule the world if I looked like that. So I set out to look like that. Nothing less. And I did rule it in a sense. My first confirmation that I had made some sort of impression started out in London where I have a friend who was a cinema cleaner, and I said to him one day, "Do you like your job?" "Yes," he said. And I said, "That means you like the people on your right and left you talk to when you're putting right the carpets in the cinema?" He said, "Yes, we often go to a neighboring cafe after work and we talk." And I said, "What about?" And he answered, "You."

I was always under attack when I lived in London, as the English treasure their indignation and will stand with their faces six inches away and say, "Who the hell do you think you are?" Americans treasure their optimism. I was standing on Third Avenue when a black gent went by and when he saw me he said, "My, you sure got it all on today!" But he was laughing, and so I laughed and he was funny and amused by me, not indignant at all. I don't know why the English get so indignant about things. When I was on television in England people said, "I saw that old fool on television—and I've got more sense than he—they should ask me to be on television. But here when the American audience sees you on T.V. not once but twice, they say, "When I saw him the first time I thought he must be mad. But he's been on television again—he must be somebody." And

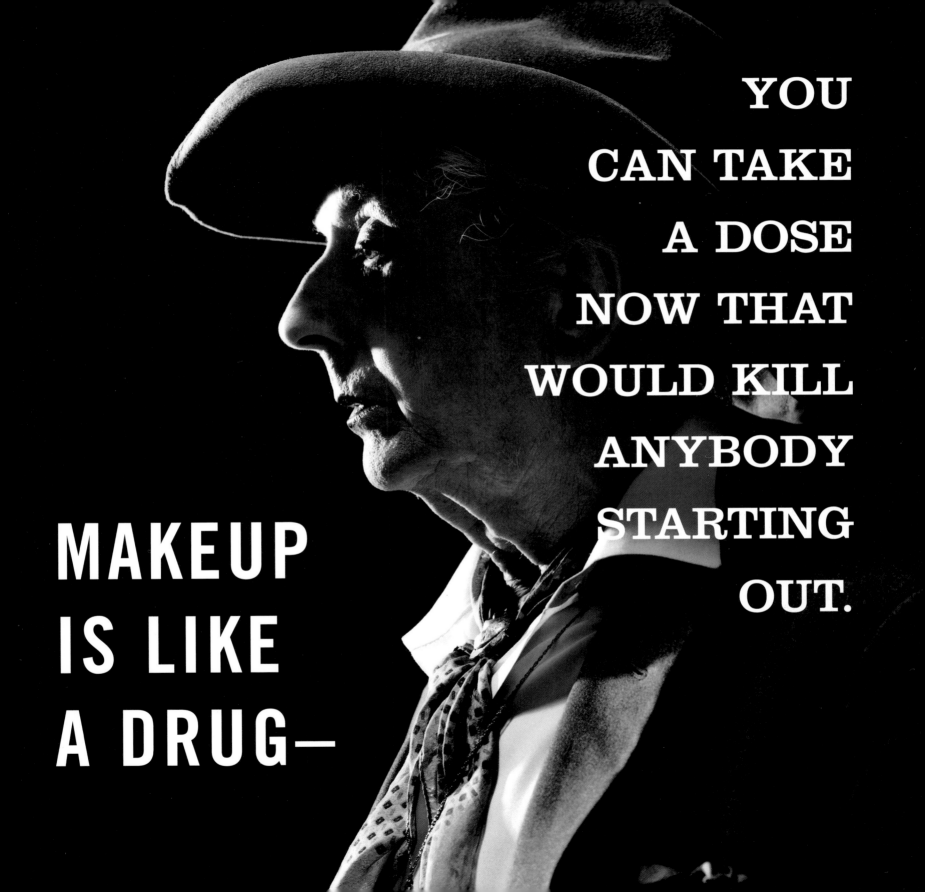

MAKEUP
IS LIKE
A DRUG—

YOU
CAN TAKE
A DOSE
NOW THAT
WOULD KILL
ANYBODY
STARTING
OUT.

they cross the road at the risk of losing their own lives in order to say, "We saw you on television!" And their faces are glowing, and it's all you can do to refrain from saying, "Bless you, child."

Nevertheless, the young people in England do like me because I annoy their parents. And the young always have had the same problem: how to rebel and conform at the same time. By rebelling against their parents and conforming to one another, they've managed to become all exactly alike. I suppose I am a kind of role model, but role models are something I disapprove of, because they enthrall the present to the past. And they entrap, not to say poppetize, the great to the less.

In fact, I represent something of a puzzle to other generations. The boys who I meet in the street say, "Why'd you do it? Do you meet more men like that?" The answer was, no, because no men would speak to you with the whole street watching. Those boys couldn't undertand that I wanted to rule the world. They wore just enough makeup to attract men but pass as somebody's nephew—but I was nobody's nephew. And that was a mystery to them. I wore men's clothes, of course, or rather clothes that could be bought at schoolboy shops by my parents. I had no money for anything more extravagant, a mere half-crown for pocket money. I did wear women's clothes one day. I thought I would try it and see what happened. And you could only say the experiment was a success, because I passed absolutely without notice. I wore shoes with fairly high heels, I wore stockings. I wore a black dress and an evening cloak and my own hair because women did have short hair, and makeup, my usual makeup. And all this passed without comment.

I think that you have to live as though you have one thing that you really want. And what I came to want was my social freedom, and for that I had to give up being rich or having

friends, or anything, really. I just lived that life because that's the only way I knew how.

Now I come from a middle-class family. My parents were middling, middle-brow, middle-class people and they lived in the suburbs. If they had lived in London inevitably they would have had a different view of me but they only knew people like themselves. I, however, have lived an urban life. I never lived in a village and hope I never will. My niece, when she went to live in Cheltenham, which is far, far away in Gloucester, gave a party of her friends and when I arrived, introduced me, saying, "And this, believe it or not, is my uncle." They were all very nice and remained unshaken. When they left, I said to her, "Well, you do know nice people." And she said rather wistfully, "Yes, but they're all people like ourselves." And they were, because English society is so structured that you cannot know anyone outside your class.

When my proclivities were first revealed, my father went on as though nothing unpleasant had happened. My mother alternatively threatened me with the outer world and tried to protect me from it. And I got stuck with the arts. Because though it may be true that artists have a peculiar appearance, it is equally true that people who look funny get stuck with the arts. My life is a mystery.

To me, clothes are one adjunct of your style. And your style is the way of telling the world who you think you are. Now I consider myself to be an elderly English gentleman of indeterminate sex. And that's how I try to represent myself. All this is a matter of context, of course. On St. Mark's Place I'm positively dowdy, compared to those rocking-horse hairdos. In fact, there's nothing you can wear on the Lower East Side which could call attention to you.

A woman once referred to my "disgusting zest for life," and that's all it is. You have a disgusting zest for life and then you want a greater kingdom. I began my career humbly enough, in a public house. In those days, public houses, or "bars" as you call them here, had opening hours at eleven a.m., then closed at half-two, and opened again in the late afternoon. The reason for this was that Lloyd George thought the workers would only go back to work when the pub shut. This particular pub offered its patrons entertainment. The proprietor didn't know what to do with the lunchtime hour and he came to me and suggested that I could go on. I said, "With what object, my good man!" "You could just talk," he said. "About what?" I said. "It doesn't matter," he said, "You needn't talk about the same thing each day." So I spoke and I spoke, then I got off the stage and sat in the pub and had a drink with the three tables of clients. But once the television program was shown, every table was taken, everyone was there with a pint of beer in one hand, crushed up against the wall. It's astonishing how notoriety changes things. That was the effect of television; it sanctified.

I tell people how to be happy; because happiness is the only thing I understand. When the sob sisters receive letters from people in the papers, saying "What am I to do about my daughter?" "How can I cope with my mother?" "How can I cope with my lover?" None of these women ever say, "Stop bothering with other people; that's all you have to do to be happy." I don't bother with other people. Oh, in heaps, I mean; not individuals. I don't sit in my room biting my nails wondering what wretched person in another street is thinking about me.  What matters is what I think about myself.

There was a man who was a comedian known as his character, "Old Mother Riley." He played the part of a cantankerous old woman and this was forever on television and on the music halls and everyone screamed with laughter because, you see,

# I WAS WEARING DRAG TO BE *ADMIRED.* EVEN POSSIBLY TO SEDUCE: YOUR SON... YOUR HUSBAND...

there is no sin like being a woman. Whenever a woman dresses as a man, nobody laughs. But when a man dresses as a woman, he is, in the eyes of the world, dressing down. This is what they couldn't understand about me—that I was serious. I was serious and I represented sin. Now sin is not well thought of in England, as we are a Puritan country. I wasn't wearing drag to be laughed at, you see; I was wearing drag to be admired. Even possibly to seduce: your son...your husband... perhaps your father! And this was a terrible thing. For drag is completely a method of seduction.

Since I present myself as someone of no particular gender, that is confusing because though barriers were falling fast—the barriers between the classes, the rich and the poor, the nationalities—the last to fall are those between the sexes. And when people used to say to me, "Are you supposed to be a man or a woman," I'd say, "Why do you ask? What were you going to suggest we should do in so limited a space?" And that only annoyed them. Of course, when I was young, women were a separate race. That said, I joined it on occasion: I played Lady Bracknell in *The Importance of Being Earnest*; and recently, I played Queen Elizabeth in *Orlando*. When English women say, "I wish I were a man," they don't mean, "I wish I could make love like a man." No, they mean, "I want to get the better of my fate." Because when you were a woman (at least until recently), all you could do was sit on a sofa with downcast eyes until someone said, "I like the look of you; I'll pay your bills for the rest of your life!" So they'd have to make the most of it somehow. It was not much of a choice.

Drag is as bizarre as it can get. No one can mistake RuPaul for a woman. He's a thing. They only want to know, "Where does he put it?" And

so it was with all great drag artists; they want every-one to know they are men in drag: not women and, perhaps, not homosexuals. When Danny LaRue became the most popular person in England, he used to stand at the top of a flight of stairs in a sequined dress sliced from the knees to the nipple, wearing high-heeled shoes. And the first thing he said to his audience was, "I bet you're wondering where I put it."

He was so popular that my sister, who was the wife of a country clergyman, would hire a coach for her friends and parishioners and go up to London to see Danny LaRue. His popularity was phenomenal. Danny was a music hall artist, and music hall art is the art of the double meaning. The greatest music hall artist ever known was Marie Lloyd. And when the Lord Chamberlain forbade her to sing her risque song, "She sits among the cabbages and peas," she simply sang instead "She sits among the lettuces and leeks." So music hall is invincible.

Barry Humphries is quite a different phenomeon. He liter-ally takes over the personage of being a woman. When you see his show it is a miracle. The first half is four little character sketches; almost little novels. The second half is Dame Edna and is a romp. Dame Edna has a husband who is impotent, a secretary who is a slut, a daughter-in-law she hates. It goes on forever. He doesn't like anybody: he hates Australians, he hates Australian women, he hates his audience. He has been known to invite a woman to hand out a box of chocolates from which he is eating and he spits in it and hands it back to her. What he hates most is that he has gotten stuck with this image, this persona. And he makes it very clear that he is not homosexual. But his drag has become malicious.

When I'd do my shows, I sometimes collect cards with questions from the audience and one said, "Do you believe in God?" I answered, hesitating, that "I wouldn't like to say any-thing to give offense." And immediately a man in the audience called out, "Why stop now?" I had to laugh, "Why indeed!"

But yes, I suppose you could say that I am about a "kinder, gentler drag," I suppose so.

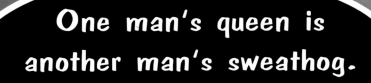

LADY BUNNY

*Tennessee-born and bred Lady Bunny, with every frosted Lee Nail and every starburst lash in place, is reigning organizer, performer and figurehead of the main event in New York's drag calendar, the summer fiesta called Wigstock. Despite her lowlife look, Bunny hails from a Southern highbrow family. When she was ten her family converted to Quakerism and spent a year in West Africa. "The best year of my life," Bunny called it in an interview in Pansy Beat. Educated at the University of Tennessee (where her father is a professor), after two years, Bunny high-tailed it to Atlanta's Georgia State and a graduate degree in go-go dancing. She came up with the name Bunny at a party when Fifties and Sixties kitsch was in. "Bunny just seemed like a good name for the very sweet and girlish-if-artsy look that I started out with. I announced myself as Bunny one night—and everybody screamed!" We chatted in a Greenwich Street coffee shop one spring day. Bunny was in denim, uncharacteristically dressed-down.*

WHEN I WAS THIRTEEN, I WENT TO CHATTANOOGA'S VERY OWN GO-GO CLUB, WHICH WAS THIS TRASHY LIP-SYNCH EMPORIUM. I TOOK ONE LOOK AT THE DRAG QUEENS AND WAS HOOKED. WHERE ELSE WOULD YOU SEE SOMEONE IN A SEQUINED GOWN WITH FALSE EYELASHES, HUGE HAIR AND TONS OF MAKEUP? DEFINITELY NOT AT THE MALL! CHATTANOOGA IS NOT EXACTLY CHOCK-FULL OF GLAMOROUS PERSONALITIES, BUT THIS PLACE HAD IT. I FELL IN LOVE WITH

them instantly; I couldn't get enough. Another place called the Cross Keys was equally exotic: there I saw a drag queen in one of those disco Grecian numbers with a cord criss-crossed over her chest to maximize her tiny hormone breasts. I've run into her ever since I was twelve years old—thrift shopping at Goodwill stores in Chattanooga.

But it really began for me in Atlanta when I started attending concerts of The Now Explosion, which was a band that didn't actually have drag in it at that time, but was part of a whole scene that included RuPaul. This was in 1982, when these nuts were putting on these outrageous theme shows. Their two female singers were very drag-like, and drag queens were encouraged to come to the show, which is how I got my start go-go dancing. Atlanta was such a fun place back then. Midtown had a strong street scene, which I'm always attracted to because I don't drive. In Atlanta at that time you would see incredible drag-queen prostitutes in halter tops, flip-flops and hot pants, walking down the street, eating a hot dog—just as sweet as could be—at all hours of the day and night. It was so trashy. It's the scene that RuPaul and I and LaHoma Van Zandt (who's a night club hostess) sprang from. That's where I got my start in show biz.

I really didn't perform until I came to New York with The Now Explosion. They usually had people along who could drive the van, but since I don't drive, they decided I could tag along as the entertainment, dressed in some ridiculous gingham outfit. My look then was so pathetic. I hadn't even mastered false eyelashes or bobby pins to keep the wig on properly! The band sure got a great deal of pleasure from seeing me eating with them at truck stops. The reactions from people!

I guess the sickest moment of all was when we were in Washington, thrift shopping, and it was very windy that day. My wig was being held on by a scarf (in my younger days I liked to feature a bow on top of my head). As it got windier and windier I decided to head back to the van. Well, I'm very much "as the crow flies"—so little sense of direction and I could not find the van. I was the only person with a set of keys, and it was start-ing to rain. There I was—I'm sure I didn't have any money at all—with the wind whipping around, in tears, in drag, in a gingham dress, knowing no one in Washington, as pathetic as you can possibly imagine. I finally found the van and eventually made it to New York. Whew!

My first performance in New York was lip-synching to "I Will Survive" at the Pyramid. I was so inexperienced that the spotlights were blinding me, and I fell off the stage. But I managed somehow to get back up, wig askew and one shoe missing, and finished the number, which was a crowd-pleaser, and I was a fixture at the Pyramid for the next six or seven years.

My role models? Well, Carol Channing can do no wrong, for one. I love Carol. She's absolute nuts, she's bonkers. But she was able to parlay that into an entire career. My number one idol is Barbara Eden. I think the most beautiful women on earth are darker, more exotic women: black or Hispanic or Asian. When a white woman has a hint of that exotic eye, like Barbara Eden, I just think you can't touch them. Now Barbara's figure never was flawless (she is very hippy), but I like voluptuous women—juicy! I think in her heyday she was gorgeous. And of course, Zsa-Zsa Gabor! I love all the Gabors, but none have the zing that Zsa-Zsa does. On a talk show she crossed her big fat leg jammed into some pump, and the audience went wild, as if she was one of the sexiest women on earth. Though she only made three movies, she has such a personality. I don't know if it's the diamonds or the wigs. She's sixty years old, but you've got to hand it to her, seeing her lift up her fat old leg, acting for all the world as if she's Marilyn Monroe. I say, "Hats off to you, honey!"

Then of course, I've always loved the witchcraft sitcoms: *I Dream of Jeannie*, *Bewitched* and Angelique, from *Dark Shadows*. I remember my eyes popping out of my head whenever [Barbara] was on the screen. All three of those shows are from a period whose styles I really appreciate: the high hair in the back, the heavy false eyelashes, liquid eyeliner and pale lips. I love that era of women's fashion. I think of that look not as retro, but as classic showgirl, "the works." It's big everything.

There's one of those bigger-than-life gals in every era: Charo, Barbie. I think it's so glamorous. Of course I was the only one in Atlanta into this look. The Dynasty look was dominant in Atlanta, the idea of passing and looking like a real woman wearing Dynasty gowns with huge shoulder pads (the last thing a drag queen needs to look more feminine, as you know!)  They love those butterfly sequined tops.

The Pyramid Club years were boozy. There were some hard-drinking days and nights. It was a very fringe scene, full of nutty kinds of stuff, and often very "in" jokes. But there was a crowd who appreciated that. It was also a place you could stop the music and do a show of considerable length that was not dance-oriented (which isn't possible in these pumping mega-discos because people are nasty, into drugs or all-night music or heavy cruising action). The Pyramid really was a nurturing scene for all kinds of performers, especially drag performers. From stand-up comedians like Happy Face, to Ethel Eikenberger (who's dead now), the Pyramid was nuts. I did everything from go-go dancing on the bar to working in the office and organizing Wigstock. It was the place to be from 1983 to 1986. There was a line around the corner every Sunday night (which was the big popular gay night). Ironically, one of the managers at the Pyramid, Hattie, never understood the importance of drag. Although gay, he had a strong tie to rock bands which were a part of the mid-Eighties East Village scene. Hattie (a.k.a. Brian Butterick) would even throw on a rock band on gay night, which would just clear the place. Pyramid was owned by a businessman, but Sister Dimension (a DJ) and Hattie were given free reign, and took all the proceeds from the door—which were considerable. It was a thriving drag scene.

"Pyramid drag" was defined by being always kooky. When I arrived the main diva was Tanya Ransom, who was a crazed heroin addict who put on a man's suit, heels, and a little eyeshadow with his own receding hair and sang his version of "Just Walk Away, Renee." Then there was Ethel, with false eyelashes down to the bottom of her nose, and glitter up to here.

She was the great-grandma of everyone there; she helped us out with makeup tips. She taught us when you put on the glue for false eyelashes to wait a minute for it to develop some tack, and how to pin your wigs on properly. There were all kinds of kooks that you wouldn't find anywhere else. It was a kind of family; a back-stabbing family of drunks. And like a family, we all got really sick of each other. Maybe that was just me, maybe no one else did, but we certainly did work very closely together.

Back then, I wasn't one of these gals that knew exactly what I wanted to do, like Lypsinka who knew exactly how she wanted to look on stage. I didn't have a clue how to get the look that I wanted. I still like a little gingham from time to time, and I used to sport bunny ears, which was a little retarded. If I see photos of myself five years ago I say, "Oh, you idiot, look at that makeup, what did you think you were doing." Now I've got the look where I want it. The makeup hardly changes; maybe a few shades of eyeshadow. I like a really lashy look. I usually put three pairs together and one on the bottom. Usually platinum blond hair, but I have gone as dark as honey blond or even red or frosted, which is such a sick look that I can't resist it sometimes. I even once had a shag wig that came with darkened roots. You know, really fool them! (Why would any-one buy a wig with roots? The trashy woman who has roots but whose hair looks a mess?) Black hair doesn't work on me because I'm fair. But I have been known to go out as Bunny's evil sister because *Bewitched* and *I Dream of Jeannie* had sisters that wore dark wigs, same makeup, but a dark wig.

Bunny is from the country but she's in the city now (though I was wearing a pinafore last Wednesday). Country singers known for huge hair were a big influence. Even now that the Sixties and Seventies are long gone, Dolly Parton's hair is enormous, and so is Reba McIntyre's. I do sing country material but I never became interested in country until I moved to New York. Actually, I don't really like country music except for the trashy stuff: Gina C. Reilly or Bobby Gentry. "Fancy" is a song I like to sing. It's about how my mama was dying and my daddy ran off, and she spent the last penny she had to buy a fancy dress for me and sent me out to prostitute myself. And I moved on up and now I'm rich and living in the city. It's my signature tune.

Bobby Gentry is one of the few artists whose country material isn't trashy that I like. In the Sixties she had R&B, country, and Las Vegas with a touch of acid thrown in there. Country has a nutty tradition too, with people like Minnie Pearl and yodeling. I adore Minnie Pearl; she's hilarious. Yodeling is outrageous, too. I do a song called "Jesus Put a Yodel in My Soul," always a crowd pleaser. I'm not a bad yodeler, I must say. I'm definitely not into "Stand by Your Man." If it's too sappy, or too mainstream, I don't like it. I like the sick stuff. I got a song the other day called "My Daddy Is a Woman." It's a little girl complaining because her daddy had a sex change operation. It's real sicky. I just bought the record and I'm gonna cover it. I do another song called "Dear Mr. Jesus" which is a little girl writing to Jesus because she saw on the news that some child was beaten up by the parents. The cli-mactic line is: "Dear Mr. Jesus, please tell me what to do, and please don't tell my mommy, but daddy hits me, too." It's so retarded. At that point in my performance I expose a drawn-on criss-crossed scar. I do so like the rot-gut trashy country stuff.

Going to school down South it's not unusual to look over and see some chick with bleached-blond hair who has obvi-ously curled it with hot rollers and is wearing caked-on foun-dation and blue eye-shadow. That really does still exist. I think the southern woman is very funny! Is it a more matriarchal society down South? I don't know. I love Dixie Carter, who described the southern woman as a "sweet, gentle lamb, really getting everything she wants." I do a take-off on that sweet southern thing, since I have never seen myself as a sexy siren, bitchy diva femme. It was always a little bit more nutty, sweet, ditsy, off-beat.

One of the things that I'm known for, I guess my biggest claim to fame, is that I'm the organizer of Wigstock. That puts me in a unique position. It's a corporation now, with shares!

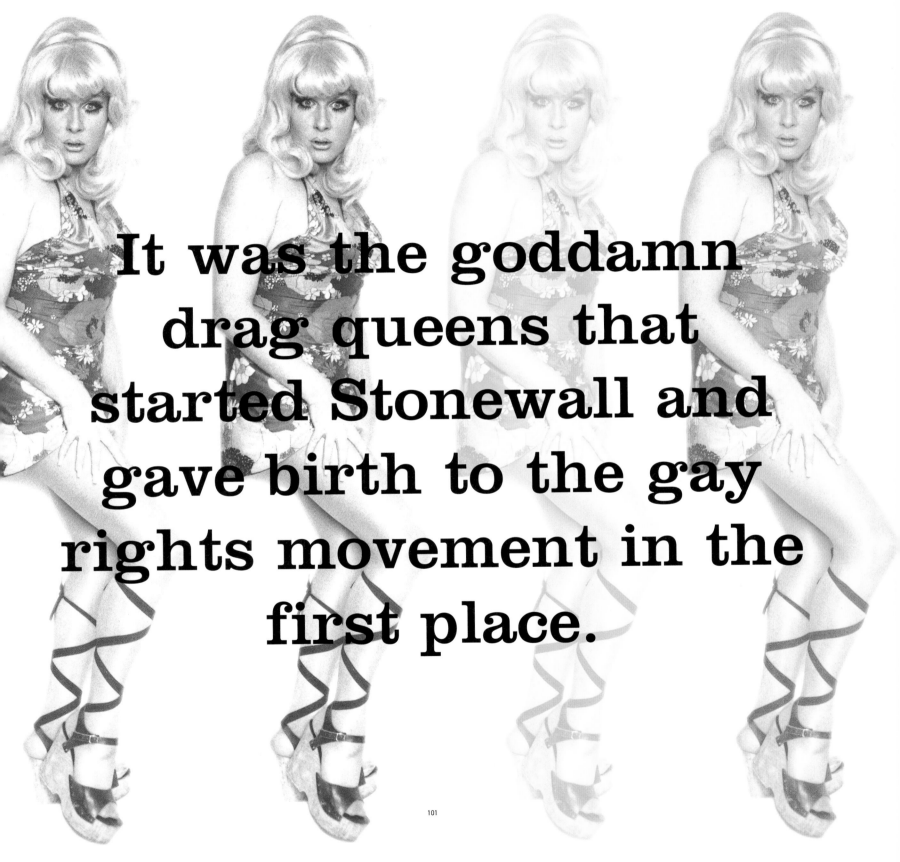

It was the goddamn drag queens that started Stonewall and gave birth to the gay rights movement in the first place.

We have a seal and a trademark! It's so hysterical. I mean, we don't have any money; but we have shares! (Do you want to buy some?) This got started one night when the Pyramid closed down and we grabbed a few six packs and headed over to Tompkin Square park to clown around on the bandshell. Hattie, Wendy Wilds (a performer at the Pyramid, who has been at Wigstock every year), and several members of the band The Flesh Tones and I suddenly thought "What if...." Wearing wigs was very much in vogue then, and they were all rock-and-roll musicians, so the idea of Wigstock was that we would have bands play. But after the first few years we gave it up because as more and more people wanted to perform it took more and more time to break-down the equipment—too many technical chores. Instead we focused more on the drag stuff. The parody between "Woodstock" and "Wigstock" faded, until now we play dance music in-between the sets. When there is no performance, we'll throw in "Aquarius." I guess the idea would have faded the next morning but I decided to go and investigate the permits, which were quite easy then, before Tompkin Square became a trouble spot after the homeless riots, and we could go on until 10:00 at night. Somehow, through the magic of Wigstock, it all happened. We certainly don't have any political clout; we don't have a ton of money, and we don't have an influential board. But somehow we have always gotten what we wanted from government agencies. One year they had to reach the Parks Commissioner in a hot tub, on vacation, before the show could go on. They really give us the runaround. Wigstock has grown and grown every year. It almost has a sort of religious devotion to it. People really do get all dressed up to make a pilgrimage to Wigstock. It's kind of a hipper version of Gay Pride Day. Now we are forced to do Wigstock every year—whether we want to or not. 25,000 people were there last year; the park is so jam-packed we couldn't even sell our tee shirts and programs. Wigstock is held on Labor Day, and last year we celebrated the tenth anniversary.

The perception of the drag explosion may be partially due

I LIK
SICK

THE
TUFF

to Wigstock. But I'd say it's largely due to RuPaul, Dame Edna, Lypsinka, Shanaynay (on *Martin*), and *Kids in the Hall*. I think drag is now perceived as an entertaining theatrical device which works. It's enjoying a vogue right now, but really, there are a lot of the same performers from the first year at Wigstock. The emphasis is still very much East Village, classic Pyramid-style drag, out-there. I like to mix bona fide dance acts which have club history, like Deee-Lite and Debbie Harry, with k.d. lang. I love the idea of having acts like that thrown into the core of this crazed fair. It makes them seem all the more ridiculous and legitimizes the whole thing in a way. Not that it needs to be legitimized, but I guess that's a testimony, that people like Debbie Harry and Deee-Lite and the B-52's want to perform.

Our strong suit is that we target a very hip audience. We don't have money, we don't have political clout—but we do have the cream of New York. We even have *Wigstock, the Movie*, filmed this past year! The footage is just amazing. I can't see why it wouldn't be as popular as *Paris Is Burning* without the somber, ultimately tragic, note of that.

Meanwhile, I'm working on a new cabaret and I've done a dance song with RuPaul's management. I'm going to Chicago to play a porn star who runs for Congress, in an independent film. I had a little cameo in *Party Girl*. I travel around a lot performing at clubs. It's a living; it's a sign of the drag thing's permanence, I guess. Someone visited South Carolina recently and overheard some teenage girls in the mall say, "You'd better work," RuPaul's refrain. So clearly drag has spread to the hinterlands. Maybe it will continue to spread, or maybe it will become overexposed and fade away and then have another renaissance. Tune in tomorrow, honey.

As a footnote to drag history, I should mention that this year Gay Pride festivities are being organized by an outside group called Stonewall 25 (rather than the usual Heritage of Pride group). They are turning the whole twenty-fifth anniversary into a kind of march, without any floats, without any music. I can't help but think that this is a desire to take the

emphasis away from the drag queens, away from the people that come in some silly costumes, or G-strings, or just come to dance. They want to present a serious face which I think is really ridiculous. It was the goddamn drag queens that *started* Stonewall and gave birth to the gay rights movement in the first place. They were the ones who said, "We're not going to take it anymore," not the credit-card Chelsea queens that work in an office. Yes, gay people are up against discrimination, AIDS, and gay-bashing. But don't they want to kick their heels up, put on some idiotic outfit and say, "we made it through another year?"

There has always been a movement among conservative gays who don't see drag as fun, who resent the drag queens as the flamboyant ones that get all the attention and media focus, who downplay all the "normal tax-paying gay people." Would they prefer that everyone march in a *suit?* Someone told me there was a clip of me on Channel 13, a clip from the San Francisco gay pride parade, put together by a conservative gay group and the question that was asked while I was on screen was: "Is *this* the image that we want to portray?" I had on some retarded pink fairy outfit with a cape and I was flapping my wings and running around. (Okay, I admit I'd taken Ecstasy!) Still, I think the parade should be cause for celebration. That brings me to another sad occasion. I was on *20/20* in a clip that was put out by some religious group trying to show how twisted gays were and how they had to be stopped. They showed footage from Wigstock the year it was in Union Square. Again I was sporting some retarded outfit. Then it cut to the women watching the video in some church, shaking their heads and digging into their purses to provide contribu-tions to get rid of me, and people like me. I just love that idea. *But I'm not going away!* They're going to have to come up with a lot of contributions to get rid of me. Actually I wanted to let them know to send the contributions directly to me—and I will retire. But if the contributions fall below $50,000 a year, I'm going to be right back out there! (Sighs deeply.) It seems so harmless to me.

**ILLE**

RENE "DILLE" DE SCHEPPER DONNED A DRESS FOR THE
FIRST TIME AT TWELVE. AT 42, "SHE" IS NOT MARRIED AND
LIVES JUST OUTSIDE OF GHENT, BELGIUM, IN THE VILLAGE OF
SAINT-MARTENS-LATENS, FAMOUS FOR ITS WRITERS AND
PAINTERS. RENE HAS BEEN CALLED "DILLE" FOR THE PAST
TWENTY-FIVE YEARS, AFTER SOMEONE WROTE "DIKKE" (FAT
PERSON) ON A CARD IN A CAFE AND THE WAITER READ IT AS
"DILLE" INSTEAD. AT 300 POUNDS, THE NAME HAS STUCK. IN
THE GARDEN BESIDE HIS COUNTRY HOUSE, THE UNCROWNED
QUEEN MOTHER OF DRAG IN EUROPE BREEDS CHICKENS,
GOATS AND SHEEP. BUT INSIDE DILLE HAS CREATED A WORLD
OF URBANE BEAUTY. AMONG HIS MORE RESPLENDENT POSSES-
SIONS, DILLE HAS CLOSETS FILLED WITH GLITTER GOWNS,
INCREDIBLE WIGS, EXOTIC MASKS, BEAUTIFUL JEWELRY,
FEATHERS, BOAS, AND HATS. IS THIS THE LIFE OF A
BARONESS? AS DILLE GRACIOUSLY EXPLAINS, "I ASPIRE TO BE
A BEAUTIFUL WOMAN—DOWN TO EVERY DETAIL."

I HAD A HAPPY CHILDHOOD,
AND FROM AN EARLY AGE WAS VERY INVOLVED WITH THE THEATER. BY TWELVE, I WAS
ACTING IN ALL SORTS OF PLAYS. DID YOU KNOW THAT IN THE SIXTIES IN BELGIUM, ALL THE FEMALE ROLES
IN THE THEATER WERE PLAYED BY MEN? SO I GOT MY THEATRICAL START AS A BOY PLAYING A GIRL, IN
DRAG. OTHER THAN THAT, I HAD A "NORMAL" TEENAGE ADOLESCENCE; I WAS EVEN INTERESTED IN GIRLS.
MY FIRST JOB WAS IN A CLOTHING FACTORY, WHERE I SEWED AND DESIGNED DRESSES. AT NINETEEN I
LEFT HOME AND FELL INTO THE PROSTITUTION WORLD IN ANTWERP WHERE I GOT A JOB AS A BARTENDER.
WHEN I DISCOVERED I COULD MAKE MORE MONEY IN THE BAR DRESSING AS A WOMAN I DIDN'T HESITATE.
AFTER ALL, MY EARLY ACTING CAREER MEANT I HAD ALREADY PLAYED AROUND WITH WOMEN'S CLOTHING.

It was nothing sexual, just fun—and it all felt good. I wasn't afraid to work in the world of prostitution; it just meant survival—and I never prostituted myself. Let's say I "animated" the customers! But I met a lot of drag queens at the time, including my friend Frieda (who's dead now). The people in the bar really just wanted someone to talk to. They talked to me about their problems at work and their miserable lives at home. They included single men and married men, and between us there was really no sexual contact. The bar was just hard work, often all night. It was a very small world. I worked there for five years, but I can say that I helped a lot of men and I definitely learned something about human nature.

My parents, of course, were horrified—and made it clear that they didn't want to see me. They knew what I was doing, even if I didn't. I still didn't realize, for example, that I was doing drag, but my feelings about it were growing stronger. A few years later I decided to create a professional drag show, and that's how my drag revue *Paris Follies* was born. For the last ten years I have been busy with it. And my drag has evolved as well: at this point, I don't always wear makeup, but I do always wear women's clothes.

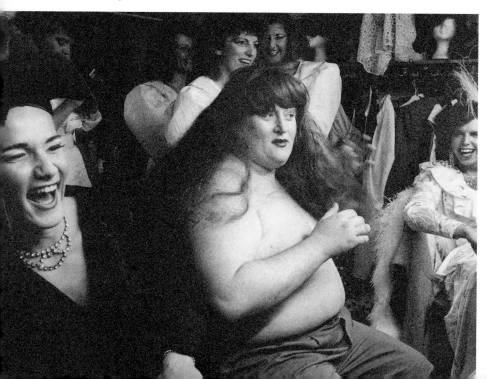

Perhaps it should be explained that a transvestite is someone who takes on the habits and dress of the opposite sex. And female behavior isn't limited to dressing in female clothing: often it involves playing a female role, with typical attitudes, styles, characteristics, and manners. But transvestites know they are men—and they want to keep it that way. Men who secretly put on female bras and panties and nylon stockings under their business suits and get some sexual kick out of it are also transvestites, but their sexual preference is usually women—many are heterosexual. But there are also transvestite men who like men. In short, there are no rules! Then there is a difference between those men and transvestites who dress up simply to accentuate their female side. Look, there is a whole scale of transvestites. The extreme end for some men is transvestitism as the first step to becoming a transsexual. First they dress as women, then they have female hormone injections, and finally they confront the final and irrevocable step—surgery.

Women who wear men's clothes and behave as men are also transvestites. Think of Marlene Dietrich in *The Blue Angel* and Liza Minnelli in *Cabaret*. But in our society women who wear trousers have it easier than men who wear dresses. The tolerance towards female transvestites is much greater. "Male women" can easily be taxi drivers, police officers or even truckers; whereas men in dresses hardly ever find work. This prejudice really forces drag into the closet, obligating men to dress up secretly. I don't know any man who has found work as a transvestite—there is really only the world of prostitution.

It's still a big taboo, though. Many transvestites remain anonymous and it's a minority who come to my shows. Most have to experience their sexuality behind closed doors. And I think it will stay an anonymous world. It is still fear, uncertainty, and shame that dominates many transvestites' lives. Many lead a sort of "double life." They don't want to "out" their true identity, in case they lose their job and family. If a woman finds out her husband is a transvestite, she may react with shock—and demand a divorce immediately. Though, in fact, many mar-

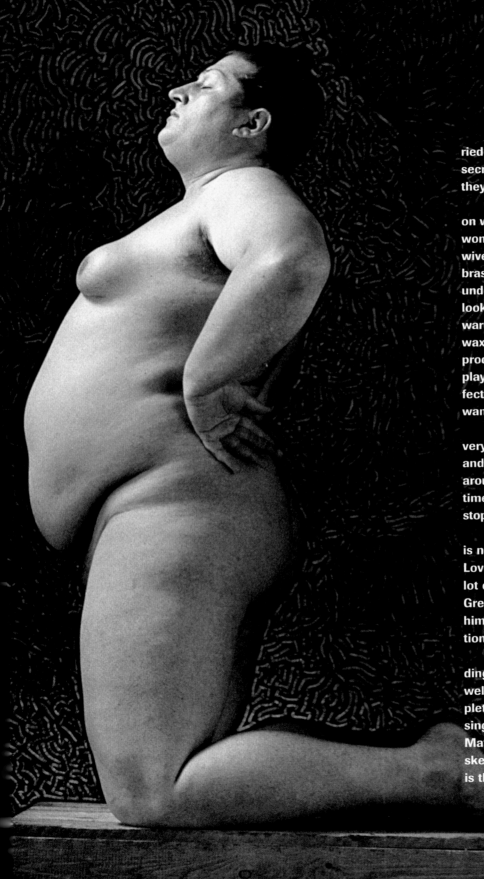

ried men are transvestites. They hide their female clothing and secretly visit clubs or bordellos. They change clothes in cars and they shop in foreign cities.

The dresses that transvestites wear vary a lot and depend on what sort of woman they want to appear like. There are classy women, sexy women, reserved women, and plain normal housewives. There are men who buy pleated skirts, cotton blouses, silk bras, slips, elegant dresses, shawls, boots, high heels and long underwear. Whatever fashion statement they make, they want to look beautiful as a woman. And drags spend a lot of time on their wardrobes. There are men who completely shave themselves or wax themselves, who spend hours choosing perfume, body care products, makeup, jewelry, and handbags. And wigs—wigs often play important roles in their lives. A lot of time is invested in perfecting female "movement." Because transvestites don't just want to look like a woman—they want to walk like women, too.

Me? I feel just fine in women's clothes. The first time it was very exciting; now it seems normal. My everyday outfit is a big skirt and a big blouse. But special fabrics or articles of clothing can be arousing in their sexual power and attractiveness. That is sometimes called a fetish, but that's a very fancy word. Where does fetish stop and transvestitism begin? The line is very slim.

But caring and love are more important to me than sex. Sex is not so important. Sex doesn't last long, love and friendship do. Love you can share with everyone, sex you can't. I haven't had a lot of relationships. I did have a seven-year relationship with a Greek seaman. He was married and had two children. I didn't see him very often, but he was a good friend and I had a good relationship with his wife and children. But it wasn't really sexual.

As for my performances, they run the gamut. I host weddings, private parties, big city affairs, and small town events as well. The show runs about two hours, and it's a real revue, complete with parodies of Nana Mouskouri (a well-known Greek singer), impressions of Diana Ross, Liza Minnelli, Mireille Mathieu, Shirley Bassey and many many more! There are also sketches and a song about my life. The star of the show definitely is the humor. Life itself—with laughter and tears. I am really

# MY FAVORITE CHARACTER IS DIVINE

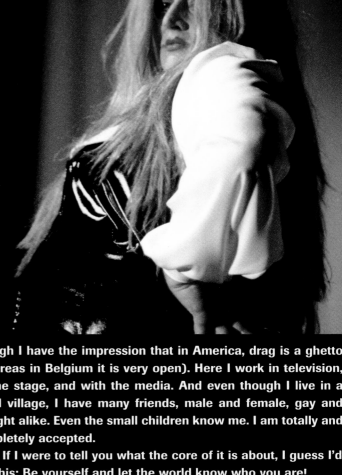

happy that I have been able to turn my life and my lifestyle into my job. Anyway, I have never cared about the reactions of the outside world. Whatever you do, you will always get comments. I just live and do exactly what I want.

What I do now is basically theater. I'm an entertainer with a show I would characterize as very "artistic." My drag radiates. It offers an appreciation and a validation. And it is a truly visual experience, not so much a sexual or power experience. I design and make almost all of my costumes, and portray a variety of characters on stage. My favorite character is Divine (I was told that I resembled him so much that he became a part of my act).

Look, I feel as strong, or as powerful, in women's clothes as in men's. Either way, you have to be yourself, and both are the "real" me. "Rene," my real name, and "Dille," my stage name, are the same person.

My family is very supportive of me. Now both my parents are deceased: my mother died in 1974 and then I lived alone with my father, who died in my arms in 1984. Sadly, neither of my parents lived to enjoy my success. But my brother and the rest of my family come to the shows. I don't need to explain myself to them, because they have been a supportive part of my evolution as a performer.

And there has definitely been an evolution in drag, and part of that is that drag is talked about more. In Belgium I certainly was the first person to dare to perform in drag publicly. I think all this is a consequence of the freedom for homosexuals that really began at the end of the war, followed by the sexual freedom in the Eighties. Now drag is truly international, and I can perform anywhere.

Though I have the impression that in America, drag is a ghetto (whereas in Belgium it is very open). Here I work in television, on the stage, and with the media. And even though I live in a small village, I have many friends, male and female, gay and straight alike. Even the small children know me. I am totally and completely accepted.

If I were to tell you what the core of it is about, I guess I'd say this: Be yourself and let the world know who you are!

# Now drag is truly international.

# HOLLY

*Holly Woodlawn is the living legend of drag who director Paul Morrissey called "a volcano mountain of energy and positivism of constant humor, resilient good nature, generous spirit and unique talent." Born Harold Ajzenberg to a Puerto Rican mother and an American-German soldier father in San Juan, Andy Warhol's last Superstar got his moniker from the Holly Golightly character in Breakfast at Tiffany's and a passing impersonation as a Woodlawn cemetery heiress. Photographed by Scavullo, Avedon and more, Holly in her heyday partied at Studio 54 with the rich and famous, starred in a dozen movies and generally lived life in the fast lane. We spoke to the indomitable, insouciant, unsinkable Holly Woodlawn, at home in the Hollywood Hills.*

MY AUTOBIOGRAPHY, *A LOWLIFE IN HIGH HEELS*, IS ALL TRUE. I AM A LOUSY LIAR. NEVER WRITE A BOOK, GIRL! I FORGOT SO MUCH, WHOLE PERIODS THAT I SIMPLY COULDN'T REMEMBER. TWO YEARS, 1970 TO 1972...BLANK! I CALLED UP ALL MY GIRLFRIENDS BUT WHAT THEY REMEMBERED AND WHAT I REMEMBERED DIDN'T MATCH. HONEY, THERE ARE CERTAIN THINGS THAT I WOULD DO, AND HONEY, THERE ARE CERTAIN THINGS THAT I WOULDN'T BE CAUGHT DOING. THEY ALL REMEMBER ME STANDING ON TOP OF TABLES SCREAMING WITH NO CLOTHES ON AND BEING BOMBED. I JUST DON'T DO THAT STUFF—HALF OF IT, YES, BUT NOT THE OTHER HALF! I SAID TO JEFFREY COPELAND ONE DAY

**Interview**

HOLLY CAME FROM MIAMI, F-L-A-,
HITCHHIKED HER WAY ACROSS THE U.S.A.,
PLUCKED HER EYEBROWS ON THE WAY,
SHAVED HER LEGS AND THEN HE WAS A SHE -
SHE SAYS, "HEY BABE, TAKE A WALK ON THE WILD SIDE."

-LOU REED FROM *"WALK ON THE WILD SIDE"*

[co-biographer], "Let's just buy a computer, move in next door, and as I remember things we'll just write them down." Little by little it happened. I would bang on his wall at three o'clock in the morning: "Oh, I just remembered something." The puzzle came together: the Holly Woodlawn story.

Every day I think about that time, my time. It really spanned twenty-five years, from the late Sixties through all of the Seventies and the early Eighties. The Eighties were when that dreaded disease came into the picture. That changed everybody's life. But let's talk about the good times—the Sixties, when I fled from Miami to New York. I was born in Puerto Rico but mainly grew up in Miami Beach. I ran far away from Miami because everyone there was either ninety-or-over or fifteen-and-under. There was no in-between. Now it's a fun town, in certain parts. But at that time there was nothing fun about Miami. I just wanted to find myself, I didn't belong there. I knew that from the time my mother took me to see this movie called *The Prodigal* with Lana Turner. Between my mother and my uncle I went to all the films. And I thought, "This is what I want to be. All these women: Hedy Lamarr, Lana Turner." I mean, this to me was what life was about. It was not doing homework or going to school and being harassed. So I saw *The Prodigal* and "Good-bye—I'm leaving." I was fifteen. My mother had this aquamarine bracelet and I hocked it and bought a ticket. The ticket only took me to Atlanta; from then on I started hitchhiking. In Atlanta I shaved my legs and plucked my eyebrows. The transition to drag had begun. And by the time I landed in New York I was a full-blown woman.

It wasn't such a radical decision, really. Everyone, all my life, kept telling me, "You are so pretty, so glamorous, so blah-blah, you should be a woman." So it was a natural thing for me to do. It started when I was a young kid—I knew that I had this female positive inside of me. But it almost destroyed my life because when I came to New York I met this guy and I thought a sex change was the answer. He saved the money up for me and I came that close. I went to Washington, D.C., and climbed onto the operating table and then I said "Nooo...No way! No, no no!" It's frightening whenever I think of it.

When we got to Atlanta, my friend Russell and I only had enough money for the bus ride. Russell was an old queen who was flawless. I worshipped her. I was this stupid little long-legged kid with bushy eyebrows. As the bus dumped us off, there was a thunder storm. We took shelter in a motel and all of a sudden lightning hit the coke machine and we both went flying. The manager felt sorry for us and let us stay that night. We were so bored—there was nothing on television—that I shaved my legs and plucked my eyebrows and next morning we went out hitchhiking. In North Carolina we got picked up by four marines and Russell had a fabulous time. But I was very shy. When we got to New York I thought Bryant Park was Central Park, that's how stupid I was. I thought,"Finally! New York is fabulous." It was frightening because we did not have any money. We met all these old queens, street people who were very nice to us. They knew we were not from "town," these two children. They took us under their wing. We hustled and sold ourselves to make ends meet, to eat and stuff.

Six months after I got to New York I met Candy Darling, about the time I found out where Greenwich Village was. ("Is that in Connecticut?" I asked someone.) We used to go hang out there. My first impression of Candy was "What a beautiful, exquisite person" and then the next impression was of a man throwing an ice cream cone in her face. She was kind of hoity-toity. Candy came from Long Island. What she would do is slip into town every weekend, go into bathrooms and get all painted and stuff. When she went back home she'd take it all off.

THE WARHOL YEARS–WHOA!
WE WERE GLAMOROUS,
FABULOUS, FLAWLESS,
WE WERE STARS–
BUT WE WERE
POVERTY-STRICKEN.

You see, in the early Sixties drag per se was against the law. If the cops wanted to harass you, female impersonation was the perfect excuse. It was against the law to wear women's clothes, even makeup. So the whole game was about passing—if you passed as a woman, you were a star. So Candy and I were stratospherically popular. Oh, those good old times! But they're not exactly the way people remember them now. People forget, for example, the real story of Stonewall. That wasn't a gay bar: it was for drag queens, after hours. The place didn't open until 2 a.m. It was a Mafia-owned thing and they paid to stay open. You would go down to the basement, knock on the door like a speakeasy from the Twenties, and let them get a peek at you. Inside, it was long bar, with two go-go boys, and as far as the music was concerned, a jukebox. So when people tell me they were there at the Stonewall, I say, "Oh yeah? And what dress were you wearing?" There was another drag place called The 10th of Always, but those two were the only places to go to after hours. Drag was just not a big thing then. If you succeeded in being truly beautiful, people would say "Oh, she's unreadable." That meant they couldn't tell if you were a man. But compared to today there was really no drag except for maybe once a year, at drag balls. There was Club 82, on Third Avenue. That was more of a Vegas thing, the girls all came out in feathers, very expensive. The waiters were lesbians, and all the girls on stage were men. It was a little small club that was around forever. It had a very good reputation, and the girls that worked there actually had jobs. "She's not walking—she's working," we used to say. I applied for a job there, but they turned me down: I looked too real. At the time I was living in Brooklyn with this guy, but as a woman, as his wife. Nobody knew, it was very strange. I led two lives. My boyfriend worked at *The New York Times*. He went to work at 5 p.m. and came home at 3 a.m. What he would do is drive me into town, and then pick me up on his way back from work. Nighttimes I would hang out with Candy Darling and Jackie Curtis and when I went back to Brooklyn, where we lived, and everyone thought I was his wife. With Candy and Jackie all we did was walk around Greenwich Village, Christopher Street, and Sixth Avenue. Then Candy got hooked with the Cafe Chino: Off, Off, Off Broadway. Andy (Warhol) came to see her in that show. It was a play like *Sunset Boulevard*. He put her in a movie and she started hanging out with Andy at Max's Kansas

# EVERYONE, ALL MY LIFE, KEPT TELLING ME "YOU ARE SO PRETTY, SO GLAMOROUS, SO BLAH-BLAH, YOU SHOULD BE A WOMAN."

City. That's where she met Jackie (Jackie was an usher at *Funny Girl* with Barbra Streisand.) We all became friends, and started hanging out at Max's. Then they did this movie *Flesh* for Andy. They became stars. So I met Andy. I really didn't get it then. Then I did *Trash* with Paul Morrissey. I joined this troupe called The Playhouse of the Ridiculous, and we did a play that Jackie wrote, and I was a chorus girl. Morrissey and

Andy came to see it. That is when they were doing *Trash*. Next thing I knew George Cukor saw it, and they tried to get me nominated for an Academy Award. Then I did *Woman in Revolt*, (which didn't really go anywhere). Then I did *Scarecrow in a Garden of Cucumber*, with Bette Midler doing the soundtrack.

The Warhol years—whoa! We were glamorous, fabulous, flawless, we were stars—but we were poverty-stricken. Everybody was living in the gutter, because Andy didn't pay us. We would go to the Factory in the afternoon to pick up invitations to parties, so at least we would eat. Uptown parties, mostly, gallery openings with, yeah, free wine and cheese. I remember lots of cheese and crackers. When *Trash* came out everyone said, "This movie made a lot of money. Why are you on welfare?" I was wondering that, too. I would go to the Factory and say, "Come on, I know I signed a release, but I'm starving, don't you have any pity?" Though in hindsight, it was okay. I knew that was what I was doing. If Andy was going to make me a star, make me famous, make me notorious, well, one hand washes the other. Before us were Viva and Edie Sedgewick, but they were rich little girls. We were desperate to be beautiful, and Andy saw that. Let Andy make the money. He took care of me. It was up to me to go on. He opened the door, the rest was up to me.

When I was doing drag, it was serious drag. Drag was not a happy word. You looked real or you didn't. My drag icons were Lana Turner, Hedy Lamarr; for Candy they were Kim Novak and Jean Harlow, and for Jackie, Lucille Ball. We loved these women. That said, it took me twenty years to get over being called a drag queen. Now it's an honor, but we had to fight for that honor. I think everybody should put on a bra and wig, panties and platforms, and scream and yell. Try it, honey, you may like it. It's America. In any other culture drag is revered, especially Japan, Kabuki and all that stuff. It has nothing to do with being disgusting or perverted. I wish they would get over that here. In England, please! The first thing they do is put on drag, it's part of tradition. Is it the puritanical garbage here that makes it marginal, or what? Anyway, after the Warhol

years I started doing clubs, I started a group called The Stilettos, where Debbie Harry was one of the back-up girls. It specialized in music from the Sixties: The Supremes, all that. I went to the clubs to get bookings and they said, "We want you but not the girls." So I did nightclub work for ten years. Then Studio 54 opened. Once that opened you either moved in or were thrown out. So I moved in. I was there for three years, 1976-1979. Lots of cocaine, fabulous people, dancing and stuff. So much money, I couldn't believe it. During that time I was a little party girl. A few years later everybody combusted. It finally caught up. In 1980 I did a couple plays with Divine. During the Eighties I didn't do very much. In 1987, when Andy died, I sort of ceased. I had a friend in L.A., so I packed two bags and came here. When I moved from Miami to New York I had fourteen dollars; when I went to L.A. I had twelve.

Right now, I don't dress except for special occasions—and for vast sums of money. Right now, I am wearing a pair of shorts, a tank top, my hair is pulled back, and I am a man. When I am going to a party, I am Holly Woodlawn, painted and in heels. Now nobody looks like that normally. I'm lazy, but if I have the razor, or the time, I do my legs or my nails. I don't think too much about it. I don't go out of my way to doll up if I'm only going to the corner. Look, drag is an occupation. What it does is it gets you noticed. Put on a pair of heels; try it. It takes your head somewhere else.

When men know that you're not a woman, I find that a lot of straight men go nuts. In a positive way, they like it. It's another whole thing that they don't understand. All that sexual shit. Women always are positive and can deal with it. It's the men that are uncomfortable. I'm glad for the whole change in drag. Especially for young kids: they don't have to think of sex change operations. They can run around in a dress until they're older. That used to be a big decision. Now it's fun, it's theater, it's wonderful. It's not something that is looked down upon anymore. Now it's like "Fuck you!" It doesn't matter. Oh boy, what a life I had, though. And when Jeffrey said "Oh, a low life in high heels!" I knew that we had to call my book that.

# DRAG

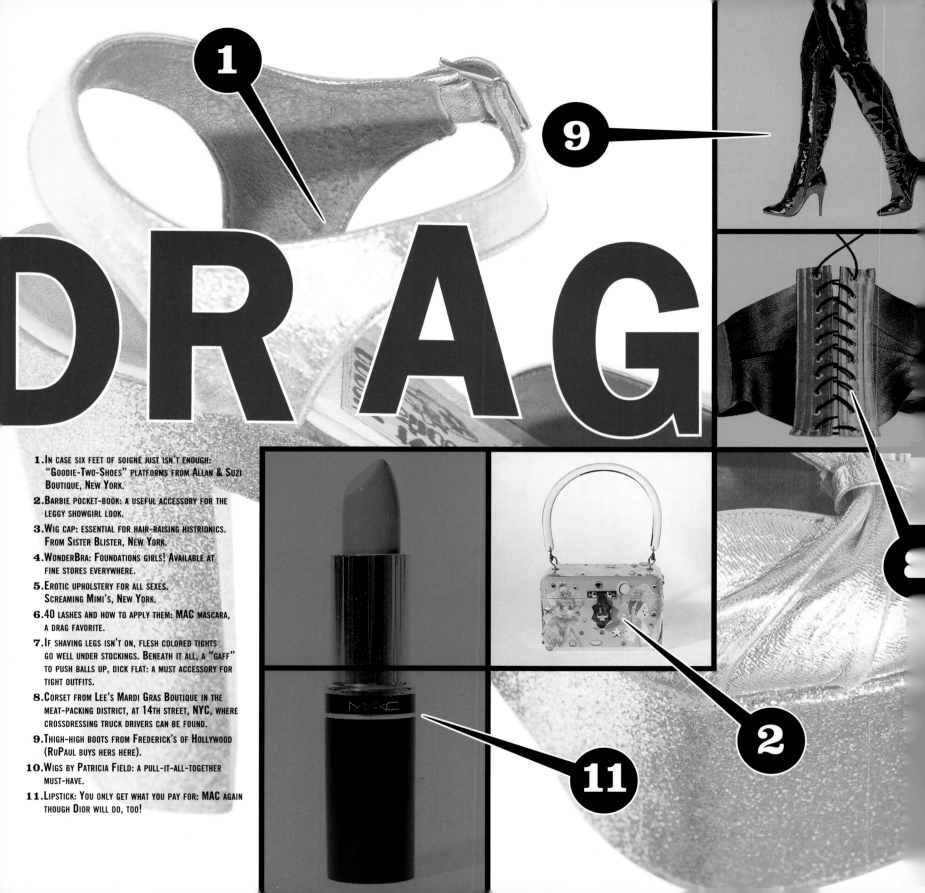

1. In case six feet of soigné just isn't enough: "Goodie-Two-Shoes" platforms from Allan & Suzi Boutique, New York.

2. Barbie pocket-book: a useful accessory for the leggy showgirl look.

3. Wig cap: essential for hair-raising histrionics. From Sister Blister, New York.

4. WonderBra: Foundations girls! Available at fine stores everywhere.

5. Erotic upholstery for all sexes. Screaming Mimi's, New York.

6. 40 lashes and how to apply them: MAC mascara, a drag favorite.

7. If shaving legs isn't on, flesh colored tights go well under stockings. Beneath it all, a "gaff" to push balls up, dick flat: a must accessory for tight outfits.

8. Corset from Lee's Mardi Gras Boutique in the meat-packing district, at 14th street, NYC, where crossdressing truck drivers can be found.

9. Thigh-high boots from Frederick's of Hollywood (RuPaul buys hers here).

10. Wigs by Patricia Field: a pull-it-all-together must-have.

11. Lipstick: You only get what you pay for: MAC again though Dior will do, too!

# SHOPPING GUIDE

## ATLANTA, GA
### SUPRA NATURAL STYLE SHOW
Drag performances and fashion show that showcases diverse design philosophies. June
### HOTLANTA
Highlighted by the Elusive Street Dance, Hotlanta features a day of partying for gays and lesbians. August

## BOSTON, MA
### LESBIAN & GAY PRIDE DAY
A parade that has been around for 25 years with a large drag showcase. June

## LOS ANGELES, CA
### CHRISTOPHER STREET FESTIVAL
The annual gay pride event in Los Angeles. June
### LA PLAZA BAR DRAG REVIEW
A nightclub with a weekly Drag Review covering contemporary drag accoutrements and drag performance. Weekly
### QUEEN MARY SHOW BAR
A traditional drag stage show. Nightly
### IMPERIAL COURT CORONATION
A formal theme and period drag event marking the changing of the elected officials of the Imperial Court and sponsored by the Imperial Court of Los Angeles. The Imperial Court is a nationwide fundraising organization giving to AIDS support, and other socially oriented projects. November

## MIAMI, FL
### WHITE PARTY WEEK
A Health Crisis Network annual fundraiser held at the Villa Vizcaya. Last Sunday in November
### TEA DANCES
Late afternoon drinking and dancing at the Club Amnesia. Sundays, October–May
### BITCH FIGHT
An unruly and old-fashioned annual drag competition started in 1994. May
### MONDAY NIGHT DRAG REVIEW
Latin Drag show–mostly glitter and feather boas–at the Barrio Restaurant. Monday nights

## NEW YORK
### WIGSTOCK
Annual drag festival attended by some 20,000 people celebrating drag and drag culture. Founded by Lady Bunny. Labor Day
### BASTILLE DAY
An irreverent celebration of Marie Antoinette and her demise held at Restaurant Florent. Plenty of drag, both contemporary and period. July 14
### JACKIE 60
A club known for its outrageous style and theme nights that often include drag. Weekly
### MISS FIRE ISLAND BEAUTY PAGEANT
A summertime beauty pageant parody. September
### NIGHT OF 1000 GOWNS
A theme and period drag event marking the changing of the elected officials of the Imperial Court and sponsored by the Imperial Court of New York. March

## PORTLAND, OR
### LA FEMME MAGNIFIQUE
A drag beauty pageant. Labor Day
### DARCELLE FIFTEEN
A female impersonation show bar with a proud tradition of drag performance and review. Nightly
### THE IMPERIAL SOVEREIGN ROSE COURT CORONATION
A formal theme and period drag event marking the changing of the elected officials of the Imperial Court and sponsored by the Imperial Court of Los Angeles. This coronation pays special tribute to the rose because Oregon is the rose state. October

### SAN ANTONIO, TX
**TEXAS "T" PARTY**
A TEXAS-STYLE GAY AND LESBIAN CONVENTION. MARCH

### SAN DIEGO, CA
**IMPERIAL COURT CORONATION**
A FORMAL THEME AND PERIOD DRAG EVENT MARKING THE CHANGING OF THE ELECTED OFFICIALS OF THE IMPERIAL COURT AND SPONSORED BY THE IMPERIAL COURT OF LOS ANGELES. AUGUST

### SAN FRANCISCO, CA
**LESBIAN & GAY FREEDOM DAY**
A GAY PRIDE EVENT WITH LOTS OF LEATHER AND DRAG. LAST SUNDAY IN JUNE
**PINK SATURDAY**
THE NIGHT PRECEDING THE LESBIAN & GAY FREEDOM DAY LISTED ABOVE. MOSTLY LESBIAN. LAST SATURDAY IN JUNE
**IMPERIAL COURT CORONATION OF SAN FRANCISCO**
A FORMAL THEME AND PERIOD DRAG EVENT MARKING THE CHANGING OF THE ELECTED OFFICIALS OF THE IMPERIAL COURT AND SPONSORED BY THE IMPERIAL COURT OF LOS ANGELES. FEBRUARY
**CASTRO STREET FAIR**
A STREET FAIR AND GENERAL GAY COMMUNITY CELEBRATION. OCTOBER 2
    **DORE ALLEY STREET FAIR**
    CHAPS ENTHUSIASTS UNITE FOR A DAY OF LEATHER, ART, AND ENTERTAINMENT. A STREET FAIR AND GENERAL GAY COMMUNITY CELEBRATION. AUGUST
    **FOLSOM STREET FAIR**
    A FAIR WITH MUSIC AND COMEDY. A STREET FAIR AND GENERAL GAY COMMUNITY CELEBRATION. LAST WEEKEND IN SEPTEMBER

### WACO, TX
**MONA MADNESS**
AIDS BENEFIT THAT INCLUDES PRODUCTION NUMBERS, FEMALE IMPERSONATION AND GENERAL WOOP. SEPTEMBER

### SYDNEY, AUSTRALIA
**SLEAZE BALL**
AN ANYTHING-GOES CELEBRATION OF GAY AND LESBIAN LIFE, DRAGS, LEATHER AND ANY COMBINATION THEREOF. OCTOBER

### TORONTO, CANADA
**IMPERIAL COURT CORONATION OF TORONTO**
A FORMAL THEME AND PERIOD DRAG EVENT MARKING THE CHANGING OF THE ELECTED OFFICIALS OF THE IMPERIAL COURT AND SPONSORED BY THE IMPERIAL COURT OF LOS ANGELES. OCTOBER

### LONDON, ENGLAND
**SEX ADDICTS BALL**
THIS EVENT CELEBRATES EVERY KIND OF SEXUAL OBSESSION. THE AIM IS FUN, AND THE RESULT IS A VISUAL DISPLAY OF MEN AS WOMEN, WOMEN AS MEN, MEN AS CHILDREN, WOMEN AS GODDESSES, YOU NAME IT. SEPTEMBER
**PORTCHESTER HALL DRAG BALL**
A LONG-RUNNING, ANNUAL NOTTING HILL GATE EVENT FEATURING A GREAT FANFARE OF DRAG. SEPTEMBER

### PARIS, FRANCE
**FASHION WEEK**
MANY OF THE COUTURE DESIGNERS-GAULTIER, VIVIENNE WESTWOOD, THIERRY MUGLER, MARTINE SITBON-INVITE DRAG QUEENS ON THE RUNWAY BEFORE OR AFTER THEIR SHOWS. OFTEN SEEN AT PARTIES AND BACKSTAGE, DRAG QUEENS ARE PART AND PARCEL OF THE FASHION WORLD. MARCH AND OCTOBER

# DRAG FI

FILMS ARE ARRANGED BY DATE, TITLE, COUNTRY OF ORIGIN, DIRECTOR (WHEN NOTEWORTHY) AND PRINCIPAL ACTOR(S)/ACTRESS(ES) IN DRAG. LISTINGS INDICATE MEN DRESSING AS WOMEN. WHEN A GENDER SWITCH INDICATES A WOMAN DRESSING AS A MAN IT IS NOTED BY AN ASTERISK (*) FOLLOWING THE FILM.

| Date | Title |
|------|-------|
| 1914 | *A Florida Enchantment* (US) Edith Storey* |
| 1914 | *The Masquerader* (US) Charlie Chaplin |
| 1914 | *A Busy Day* (US) Charlie Chaplin |
| 1915 | *A Woman* (US) Charlie Chaplin |
| 1915 | *Miss Fatty's Seaside Lovers* (US) Fatty Arbuckle |
| 1917 | *The Countess Charming* (US) Julian Eltinge |
| 1917 | *The Clever Mrs. Carfax* (US) Julian Eltinge |
| 1918 | *The Widow's Might* (US) Julian Eltinge |
| 1919 | *Yankee Doodle in Berlin* (US) Bothwell Browne |
| 1919 | *I Don't Want to Be a Man* (Germany) Dir. Ernst Lubitsch, Ossi Oswalda* |
| 1919 | *Miss Crusoe* (US) Virginia Hammond* |
| 1920 | *An Adventuress* (US) Julian Eltinge, Rudolph Valentino (also released as *The Isle of Love*) |
| 1920 | *Hamlet* (Denmark) Asta Nielsen* |
| 1924 | *The Thief of Bagdad* (US) Douglas Fairbanks |
| 1925 | *Charley's Aunt* (US) Syd Chaplin, Brandon Thomas (also 1926, 1931, 1940, 1942, 1952) |
| 1925 | *Man on the Box* (US) Syd Chaplin |
| 1925 | *The Sea Squawk* (US) Harry Langdon |
| 1926 | *Pay as you Exit* (US) Our Gang |
| 1928 | *The Chaser* (US) Harry Langdon |
| 1928 | *Beggars of Life* (US) Louise Brooks* |
| 1929 | *That's My Wife* (US) Stan Laurel, Oliver Hardy |
| 1930 | *Another Fine Mess* (US) Stan Laurel, Oliver Hardy |
| 1930 | *Charley's Aunt* (US) Charlie Ruggles |
| 1931 | *Morocco* (US) Marlene Dietrich* |
| 1931 | *Palmy Days* (US) Eddie Cantor |
| 1931 | *Maid to Order* (US) Julian Eltinge |
| 1932 | *Blonde Venus* (US) Marlene Dietrich* |
| 1933 | *Viktor und Viktoria* (Germany) Renate Muller* |
| 1933 | *The Warrior's Husband* (US) Ernest Truex |
| 1933 | *Queen Christina* (US) Greta Garbo* |
| 1933 | *Twice Two* (US) Stan Laurel, Oliver Hardy |
| 1934 | *Hollywood Party* (US) Jimmy Durante |
| 1935 | *First a Girl* (UK) Jessie Matthews* |
| 1935 | *Sylvia Scarlett* (US) Katharine Hepburn* |
| 1936 | *Stars on Parade* (US) (Old Mother Riley) Arthur Lucan |
| 1936 | *The Devil Doll* (US) Lionel Barrymore |
| 1936 | *Our Gang Follies of 1936* (US) |
| 1937 | *Wings of the Morning* (UK) Annabella* |
| 1938 | *Bringing up Baby* (US) Cary Grant |
| 1939 | *Old Mother Riley M.P.* (UK) Arthur Lucan |
| 1939 | *The Amazing Mr. Williams* (US) Melvyn Douglas |
| 1940 | *Chumps at Oxford* (US) Stan Laurel |
| 1940 | *Charley's Big-Hearted Aunt* (US) Arthur Askey |
| 1940 | *If I Had My Way* (US) Julian Eltinge |
| 1940 | *Turnabout* (US) Carole Landis, John Hubbard |
| 1940 | *Seven Sinners* (US) Marlene Dietrich* |
| 1941 | *Sullivan's Travels* (US) Veronica Lake* |
| 1941 | *Charley's Aunt* (US) Jack Benny |
| 1941 | *Old Mother Riley's Ghosts* (UK) Arthur Lucan |
| 1941 | *Love Crazy* (US) William Powell |
| 1942 | *Babes on Broadway* (US) Mickey Rooney |
| 1943 | *The Chance of a Lifetime* (US) George Stone, Chester Morris |
| 1943 | *Old Mother Riley Detective* (UK) Arthur Lucan |
| 1945 | *Boy! What a Girl* (US) Dir. Arthur Leonard, Tim Moore |
| 1947 | *Road to Rio* (US) Bob Hope |
| 1949 | *Laramie* (US) Smiley Burnette |
| 1949 | *Old Mother Riley's New Venture* (UK) Arthur Lucan |

# OGRAPHY

|  |  |
|------|------|
| 1949 | *I Was a Male War Bride* (US) Cary Grant |
| 1949 | *Kind Hearts and Coronets* (UK) Alec Guinness |
| 1950 | *Old Mother Riley, Headmistress* (UK) Arthur Lucan |
| 1950 | *At War with the Army* (US) Jerry Lewis |
| 1950 | *The Rabbit of Seville* (US) Bugs Bunny, Elmer Fudd |
| 1951 | *The Lemon Drop Kid* (US) Bob Hope |
| 1952 | *Old Mother Riley Meets the Vampire* (UK) Arthur Lucan |
| 1952 | *The Crimson Pirate* (US) Burt Lancaster |
| 1952 | *Where's Charley?* (US) Ray Bolger |
| 1953 | *Glen or Glenda* (US) Dir. Ed Wood, Jr. |
| 1954 | *The Belles of St. Trinian's* (UK) Alastair Sim |
| 1957 | *Man of a Thousand Faces* (US) James Cagney |
| 1957 | *What's Opera Doc?* (US) Bugs Bunny |
| 1957 | *Blue Murder at St. Trinian's* (UK) Alastair Sim |
| 1958 | *South Pacific* (US) Mitzi Gaynor*, Ray Walston |
| 1959 | *Some Like It Hot* (US) Jack Lemmon, Tony Curtis |
| 1959 | *The Mouse That Roared* (UK) Peter Sellers |
| 1960 | *Carry on Constable* (UK) Charles Hawtrey |
| 1960 | *High Time* (US) Bing Crosby |
| 1960 | *Psycho* (US) Dir. Alfred Hitchcock, Tony Perkins |
| 1961 | *Homicidal* (US) Dir. William Castle, Jean Arless* |
| 1963 | *Dr. No* (UK) Sean Connery |
| 1963 | *Flaming Creatures* (US) Dir. Jack Smith, all drag cast |
| 1964 | *Women...Oh, Women* (Japan) Documentary |
| 1964 | *Disorder* (France) Louis Jourdan |
| 1964 | *Harlot* (US) Dir. Andy Warhol, Mario Montez |
| 1965 | *Screen Test # 2* (US) Dir. Andy Warhol, Mario Montez |
| 1965 | *Hedy* (US) Dir. Andy Warhol, Mario Montez |
| 1965 | *More Milk Yvette* (US) Dir. Andy Warhol, Mario Montez |
| 1965 | *Paris Secret* (France) |
| 1966 | *A Funny Thing Happened on the Way to the Forum* (US) Zero Mostel |
| 1966 | *The Glass Bottom Boat* (US) Paul Lynde |
| 1966 | *Cul-De-Sac* (UK) Dir. Roman Polanski, Donald Pleasence |
| 1966 | *The Chelsea Girls* (US) Dir. Andy Warhol, Mario Montez |
| 1967 | *The Tiger Makes Out* (US) Eli Wallach |
| 1967 | *The Comedians* (UK) Alec Guinness |
| 1967 | *Mondo Balordo* (Italy) |
| 1967 | *Bedazzled* (UK) Dudley Moore, Peter Cook |
| 1967 | *Thoroughly Modern Millie* (US) James Fox |
| 1967-8 | *Andy Warhol's Flesh* (US) Dir. Paul Morrissey, Jackie Curtis, Candy Darling |
| 1967-8 | *Lonesome Cowboys* (US) Dir. Andy Warhol |
| 1968 | *The Black Lizard* (Japan) Dir. Kinji Fukasaku |
| 1968 | *The Queen* (US) Documentary |
| 1968 | *No Way to Treat a Lady* (US) Rod Steiger |
| 1968 | *Eat Your Makeup* (US) Divine |
| 1968 | *The Ugliest Girl in Town* (US) TV Series |
| 1969 | *Coming Apart* (US) Rip Torn |
| 1969 | *Nude Inn* (US) Dir. Richard Fontaine, Miss Glory Holedon |
| 1969 | *The Damned* (Italy) Dir. Luchino Visconti, Helmut Berger |
| 1969 | *Fellini Satyricon* (France/Italy) Dir. Federico Fellini, Alain Cuny |
| 1969 | *The Magic Christian* (UK) Peter Sellers |
| 1970 | *Mondo Trasho* (US) Divine |
| 1970 | *Multiple Maniacs* (US) Divine |
| 1970 | *Dinah East* (US) Jeremy Stockwell |
| 1970 | *Andy Warhol's Trash* (US) Dir. Paul Morrissey, Holly Woodlawn |
| 1970 | *Myra Breckenridge* (US) Rex Reed |

A CINEVISTA RELEASE "BLACK LIZARD" NOVEL BY RAMPO EDOGAWA

| | | | |
|---|---|---|---|
| 1970 | *The Kremlin Letter* (US) George Sanders | 1975 | *Dog Day Afternoon* (US) Dir. Sidney Lumet, Chris Sarandon |
| 1970 | *The Christine Jorgensen Story* (US) John Hansen | 1976 | *Car Wash* (US) Antonio Fargas |
| 1970–4 | *The Flip Wilson Show* (US) TV Series, Flip Wilson | 1976 | *The Pink Panther Strikes Again* (US) Peter Sellers |
| 1971 | *Luminous Procuress* (US) The Cockettes | 1976 | *Pleasure at Her Majesty's* (UK) Monty Python's Flying Circus |
| 1971 | *Tricia's Wedding* (US) The Cockettes | 1976 | *The Missouri Breaks* (US) Marlon Brando |
| 1971 | *Fortune and Men's Eyes* (Canada) Michael Greer | 1976 | *The Ritz* (US) Jerry Stiller |
| 1971 | *Scarecrow in a Garden of Cucumbers* (US) The Cockettes | 1977 | *Outrageous* (Canada) Craig Russell |
| 1971 | *And Now For Something Completely Different* (UK) Monty Python's Flying Circus: John Cleese, Eric Idle, Graham Chapman, Terry Gilliam, Michael Palin, Terry Jones | 1977 | *El Lugar sin Limites* (Mexico) Dir. Arturo Ripstein, Lucha Villa |
| 1971 | *Everything You Always Wanted to Know About Sex* (US) Dir. Woody Allen | 1978 | *House Calls* (US) Walter Matthau |
| 1971 | *Women in Revolt* (US) Dir. Paul Morrissey, Jackie Curtis, Candy Darling, Holly Woodlawn | 1978 | *In The Year of Thirteen Moons* (Germany) Dir. Rainer Werner Fassbinder |
| 1972 | *Our Miss Fred* (UK) Danny LaRue | 1979 | *Monty Python's Life of Brian* (UK) Monty Python's Flying Circus |
| 1972 | *Carry On Camping* (UK) Charlie Hawtrey | 1979 | *The Secret Policeman's Ball* (UK) Monty Python's Flying Circus |
| 1972 | *Cabaret* (US) Liza Minnelli* | 1979 | *La Cage aux Folles* (France/Italy) Michel Serrault |
| 1972 | *Dr. Jeckyl and Sister Hyde* (US) | 1979 | *Third Generation* (Germany) Dir. Rainer Werner Fassbinder |
| 1972 | *Fuzz* (US) Burt Reynolds, Jack Weston | 1979–81 | *The Benny Hill Show* (UK) BBC TV Series, Benny Hill |
| 1972 | *I Want What I Want* (UK) Anne Heywood* | 1980–82 | *Bosom Buddies* (US)(TV Series) Tom Hanks, Peter Scolari |
| 1972 | *Pink Flamingos* (US) Divine (nee Glen Milstead) | 1981 | *La Cage aux Folles II* (France) Michel Serrault |
| 1972–3 | *M*A*S*H* (US) TV Series | 1981 | *Polyester* (US) Dir. John Waters, Divine, Tab Hunter |
| 1973 | *Theatre of Blood* (UK) Vincent Price | 1982 | *Querelle* (Germany) Dir. Rainer Werner Fassbinder |
| 1974 | *Monty Python and the Holy Grail* (UK) Monty Python's Flying Circus | 1982 | *Private Popsicle* (Israel) |
| 1974 | *Valerie* (US) Documentary | 1982 | *Come Back to the Five and Dime Jimmy Dean, Jimmy Dean* (US) Cher* |
| 1974 | *Freebie and the Bean* (US) Christopher Morley | 1982 | *The Secret Policeman's Other Ball* (UK) Monty Python's Flying Circus |
| 1974 | *Thunderbolt and Lightfoot* (US) Jeff Bridges, Clint Eastwood | | |
| 1974–94 | *Saturday Night Live* (US) TV Series | | |
| 1975 | *Rocky Horror Picture Show* (US) Tim Curry | | |
| 1975 | *Female Trouble* (US) Divine | | |

| | | |
|---|---|---|
| 1982 | *Monty Python Live at the Hollywood Bowl* (UK) Monty Python's Flying Circus | |
| 1982 | *Victor/Victoria* (US) Robert Preston, Julie Andrews* | |
| 1982 | *Tootsie* (US) Dir. Sidney Pollock, Dustin Hoffman | |
| 1982 | *The World According to Garp* (US) John Lithgow | |
| 1983 | *Monty Python's Meaning of Life* (UK) Monty Python's Flying Circus | |
| 1983 | *Easy Money* (US) Rodney Dangerfield | |
| 1983 | *Yellowbeard* (US) Graham Chapman | |
| 1983 | *Psycho II* (US) Anthony Perkins | |
| 1983 | *Privates on Parade* (US) John Cleese | |
| 1983 | *Private School* (US) Jonathan Price, Matthew Modine, Michael Zorek | |
| 1983 | *Vestida de Azul* (Spain) Documentary | |
| 1983 | *Liquid Sky* (US) Anne Carlisle* | |
| 1983 | *Smokey and the Bandit, Part III* (US) | |
| 1984 | *Crimes of Passion* (US) Dir. Ken Russell | |
| 1984 | *Yentl* (US) Barbra Streisand* | |
| 1985 | *The Wedding* (France/Italy) | |
| 1985 | *Lust in the Dust* (US) Divine | |
| 1985 | *Kiss of the Spider Woman* (US) Dir. Hector Babenco, William Hurt | |
| 1985 | *What Sex Am I?* (US)(TV Documentary) Dir. Lee Grant | |
| 1985 | *La Cage aux Folles III* (France) Michel Serrault | |
| 1985 | *A Man Like Eva* (Germany) Eva Mattes* | |
| 1986 | *Her Life as a Man* (US) (TV Movie)* | |
| 1986 | *Across the Rubicon* (South Africa) Pieter-Dirk Uys | |
| 1986 | *Second Serve* (US)(CBS TV) Vanessa Redgrave* | |
| 1987 | *Torch Song Trilogy* (US) Harvey Fierstein | |
| 1987 | *The Last Song* (Thailand) Dir. Pisam Akuraserani | |
| 1988 | *Big Top Peewee* (US) Peewee Herman (nee Paul Rubens) | |
| 1989 | *Nuns on the Run* (UK) Eric Idle, Robbie Colterene | |

| | |
|---|---|
| 1989-93 | *The Dame Edna Experience* (UK) (TV Series), Barry Humphries |
| 1990 | *Paris Is Burning* (US) Dir. Jennie Livingston, Documentary |
| 1991 | *On Patrol* (US) (TV Movie) |
| 1992 | *Vegas in Space* (US) Dir. Philip Ford, all drag cast |
| 1992 | *Glamazon: A Different Kind of Girl* (US) Dir. Rico Martinez, Documentary |
| 1992 | *The Brenda and Glenda Show* (US) (TV Public Access) Brenda and Glenda |
| 1992 | *Come 'N Get It* (US)(TV Public Access) |
| 1992 | *The Crying Game* (Ireland/UK) Jaye Davidson |
| 1992 | *Split* (US) International Chrysis, Documentary |
| 1992 | *Dame Edna's Hollywood* (US) (TV Series) Barry Humphries |
| 1993 | *Orlando* (UK) Tilda Swinton*, Quentin Crisp |
| 1993 | *Mrs. Doubtfire* (US) Robin Williams |
| 1993 | *Farewell My Concubine* (Hong Kong) Dir. Chen Kaige |
| 1993 | *Sex of the Stars (Le Sexe des Etoiles)* (Canada) Dir. Paul Baillargeon, Denis Mercier |
| 1994 | *Martin* (US) TV Series, Martin Lawrence |
| 1994 | *Kids in the Hall* (US) TV Series |
| 1994 | *Priscilla, Queen of the Desert* (Australia) Terence Stamp |
| 1994 | *Ed Wood* (US) Dir. Tim Burton, Johnny Depp |
| 1994 | *Just Like a Woman* (UK) Adrian Pasdar |
| 1995 | *To Wong Foo, Thanks for Everything Julie Newmar* (US) Prod. Steven Spielberg, Patrick Swayze, Wesley Snipes, John Leguiziamo |
| 1995 | *Birds of a Feather* (US) Dir. Mike Nichols |

Ackroyd, Peter. *Dressing Up*.
New York: Simon and Schuster, 1979.

Appelby, Amy, ed. *Quentin Crisp's Book of Quotations*. New York: Macmillan,1989.

Atkins, J. A. *Sex in Literature*. Vol's. I, II, III, IV.
New York: Riverrun, 1994.

Baker, Roger. *Drag: A History of Female Impersonation on the Stage.*
London: Cassell House, 1994.

Balzac, Honore de. *Sarrasine*, in Roland Barthes, *SZ*, trans. Richard Miller.
New York: Hill and Wang, 1974.

Balzac, Honore de. *Seraphita*.
New York: Hippocrene, 1990.

Baruma, Ian. *Behind the Mask: On Sexual Demons, Sacred Mothers Transvestites, etc*. New York: Pantheon, 1984.

Bell-Meterau, Rebecca. *Hollywood Androgyny*.
New York: Columbia University Press, 1985.

Benedict, Ruth. *Patterns of Culture*.
New York: Houghton Mifflin, 1989.

Bray, Alan. *Homosexuality in Renaissance England*.
London: Gay Men's Press, 1982.

Broadbent, R.J. *A History of Pantomime*.
London: Simpkin Marshall Hamilton Kent, 1901.

Bulliet, C.J. *Venus Castina: Famous Female Impersonators, Celestial and Human*.
New York: Covici Friede, 1933.

Bullough, Vern and Bonnie. *Cross Dressing, Sex and Gender*. Philadelphia: University of Pennsylvania Press, 1993.

–*Sexual Variance in Society and History*.
Chicago: University of Chicago Press, 1976.

Butler, Judith. *Gender Trouble*.
New York: Routledge, 1990.

Cocteau, Jean, and Man Ray. *Le Barbette*.
Paris: Jacques Damase, 1980.

Commondenominator, Lois, ed. *Dragazine*.
West Hollywood, CA. Published "two or three times a year while we do our nails."

Cox, Cynthia. *The Enigma of the Age: The Strange Story of the Chevalier d'Eon*.
London: Longmans Green, 1966.

Crisp, Quentin. *The Naked Civil Servant*.
New York: New American Library, 1983.

De Choisy. *The Transvestite Memoirs of the Abbe de Choisy and the Story of the Marquis-Marquise de Banneville*, trans R. H. F Scott.
London: Peter Owen, 1973.

Dickens, Homer. *What a Drag*.
New York: Quill, 1984.

de Deckert, Michel. *Madame le Chevalier d'Eon*.
Paris: Perrin, 1987.

Docter, Richard F. *Transvestites and Transsexuals: Toward a Theory of Cross-Gender Behavior*.
New York: Plenum, 1988.

Ellis, Havelock. *Studies in the Psychology of Sex*.
New York: Random House, 1936.

Everage, Dame Edna. *My Gorgeous Life*.
London: Macmillan, 1989.

Farer, Peter, ed. *Men in Petticoats: A Selection of Letters from Victorian Newspapers*.
Liverpool: Karn Publications, 1987.

Feinbloom, Deborah Heller. *Transvestites & Transsexuals*. New York: Delacorte Press, 1976.

Fielding, Henry. *The Female Husband*. (1746.)
Liverpool: University Press, 1960.

Fisher, John. *Funny Way to Be a Hero*.
London: Frederick Muller, 1973.

Flugel, J. C. *The Psychology of Clothes*.
London: Hogarth Press, 1930.

Freud, Sigmund. *Fetishism*.
New York; W.W. Norton, 1974.

Fuss, Diane. *Inside Our Lesbian Theories, Gay Theories*. Ann Arbor: University of Michigan, 1991.

Garber, Marjorie. *Vested Interests*.
New York: Routledge, 1992.

de Gautier, Theophile. *Mademoiselle de Maupin* (1835). Joanna Richardson, trans.
New York: Penguin, 1981.

Genet, Jean. *The Thief's Journal*.
New York: Grove Atlantic, 1987.

Gilbert, O.P. *Men in Women's Guise*.
London: John Lane, 1926.

Goldin, Nan. *The Other Side*.
New York; Scalo, 1993.

Judd, Ralph. *Drag Gags*.
San Francisco: Atlas Press, 1991.

Haec Vir. *Or the Womanish-Man*.
English Pamphlet, 1620.

Hic Mulier. *Or, the Man-Woman: Being a Medicine to Cure the Coltish Disease of the Staggers in the Masculines-Feminines of Our Times*.
English pamphlet, 1620.

Hirschfeld, Magnus. *Die Transvestiten*.
Berlin: Aldred Pulvermacher, 1910.

Hollander, Anne. *Seeing through Clothes*.
New York: Avon Books, 1978.

Hwang, David Henry. *M. Butterfly*.
New York: NAL, 1989.

King, Dave. *The Transvestite and the Transexual*.
Aldershot, Hants, England: Averbury, 1993.

Kirk, Kris, and Heath, eds. *Men in Frocks*.
London: Gay Men's Press, 1984.

MacKenzie, Gordene Olga. *Transgender Nation*.
Bowling Green Ohio: Green State University Popular Press, 1994.

Mander, Raymond and Joe Mitchenson. *British Music Hall: A Story in Pictures*.
London: Peter Davis, 1965.

Morris, Jan. *Conundrum*.
New York: Harcourt Brace Jovanovich, 1974.

Newton, Esther. *Mother Camp: Female Impersonation in America*.
Berkeley: University of California Press, 1979.

Nixon, Edna. *Royal Spy: The Strange Case of the Chevalier d'Eon*. New York: Reynal & Co.,1965.

Rechy, John. *City of Night*.
New York: Grove Atlantic, 1988.

Russo, Vito. *The Celluloid Closet: Homosexuality in the Movies*. New York: Harper and Row, 1987.

Savich, Evgeny. *Homosexuality, Transvestitism and Change of Sex*. London: Longmans Green, 1958.

Sernst, Earle. *The Kabuki Theatre*.
Honolulu: University Press of Hawaii, 1974.

Smith-Rosenberg, Carroll. *Disorderly Conduct: Visions of Gender in Victorian America*.
London: Oxford University Press, 1985.

Slide, Anthony. *The Great Pretenders*.
Lombard, Illinois: Wallace Homestead, 1986.

–*The Vaudevillians*.
Westport, Connecticut: Arlington House, 1981.

Stoller, Robert J. *Sex and Gender: On the Development of Masculinity and Femininity*.
London: The Hogarth Press, 1968.

–*Observing the Imagination*.
New Haven: Yale University Press, 1985.

Talamini, J. T. *Boys Will Be Girls*.
Washington, D.C.: University Press of America, 1982.

Toll, Robert. *On With the Show*.
New York: Oxford University Press, 1974.

Tyler, Parker. *Screening the Sexes: Homosexuality in the Movies*.
New York: Holt Rinehart Winston, 1972.

Underwood, Peter. *Life's a Drag*.
London: Leslie Frewin, 1974.

Werther, Ralph and Jennie June. *The Female Impersonators*.
New York: Arno Press, 1975.

Wilde, Oscar. *Salome: A Tragedy in One Act*, trans. Alfred Douglas. New York: Dover, 1967.

Worman, Martin. *Midnight Masquerade: The History of the Cockettes*. Unpublished Ph.D. thesis, New York University, 1992.

Woolf, Virginia. *Orlando: A Biography*.
New York: Penguin, 1970.

Woodlawn, Holly, with Jeff Copeland. *A Low Life in High Heels*.
New York: St. Martin's Press, 1991.

## ACKNOWLEDGMENTS

OUR THANKS TO THE FOLLOWING INDIVIDUALS WHO ASSISTED AND ADVISED US: CAROLINE HERTER, SARAH MALARKEY, AND DAVID CARRIERE, CHRONICLE BOOKS; HANNAH LEIDER, REINER DESIGN CONSULTANTS; LARRY KARDISH, MUSEUM OF MODERN ART FILM DEPARTMENT; RON MAGLIOSO, MUSEUM OF MODERN ART FILM STUDIES DEPARTMENT; ALAN HERZBERG; JENNI OLSEN, FRAMELINE; JESSE FROHMAN; LEN PRINCE; SHONNA VALESKA; MICHAEL FAZAKERLY; WOUTER DERUYTTER; LIZZIE HIMMEL; ALBERT SANCHEZ; FREDDY BERKOWITZ, *DRAGAZINE* MAGAZINE; PATRICK BAROCH, SONY CLASSICS; ANDY KARSCH, LONGFELLOW PICTURES; CHARLES GLASS; JULIAN SANDS; FLORENT RESTAURANT; SHEILA NEVINS, HBO; FRED RITCHIN, NEW YORK UNIVERSITY; AND ESPECIALLY, ALL THE SUBJECTS OF THE BOOK WHO HAVE BEEN SO GRACIOUS WITH THEIR TIME AND EXPERTISE.